SO WHAT'S
THE HURRY?

SO WHAT'S THE HURRY?

Tales from the Train

Jane Fishman

Real People Publishing

SAVANNAH, GEORGIA

If you would like to order more copies of *So What's the Hurry? Tales from the Train*, go to the independent bookstore in your town, Amazon.com or Lulu.com and search under the book title or the author's name.

Cover and book design by Tom Greensfelder.

Photos by Carmela Aliffi and Jane Fishman.

ISBN 978-1-7923-2145-0

Printed in the United States of America.

TABLE OF CONTENTS

FOR BAKER AND BENNY,
FUTURE TRAIN TRAVELERS

INTRODUCTION

TRAINS ARE A HARD SELL. We are car people. We want to throw our gear into the back of a vehicle that sits right outside our front door. We want to bring our dogs, our pillows, our blender, maybe a third or fourth pair of shoes. We like to be in charge of our outings. We don't like delays. A cow's in the middle of the train tracks? Ridiculous. Move him.

We're airplane people. Zip, zip, zip. Who has time for trains?

We're a car culture. We're entitled. That's why we have all these highways, so we can get places. Fast. Except it's not always faster. It's counter-intuitive. As it turns out, building roads increases congestion. A section of Interstate 10 in Houston is twenty-six lanes across. After it was built, the morning commute got worse in both directions, same with the eastbound in the evening. The new phrase for this is "induced traffic demand." The good news is a few years ago folks in Los Angeles, citing "induced traffic demand," voted against adding more lanes to a freeway.

Trains are old-fashioned, so nineteenth-century.

So what if nearly 85,700 people – some 31 million a year – ride the train every day.

It's not hard to see what happened with trains. Sometime in the 1950s folks in the car industry got together with folks in the oil industry and said, "Let's bypass the trains. All right, they got us out West. They expanded the country. They moved the cotton. But right now? They're not doing either of our businesses any good. They're passé. We need to sell cars. We need to sell gas. Let's build highways."

And that's what happened. In 1956 the Federal Aid Highway Act, officially called the Dwight D. Eisenhower National System of Interstate and Defense Highways, was enacted. Trains, while still carrying passengers, got nothing.

No more track. No more locomotives. No more attention. The inner cities, where most trains start and end, got nothing. It became popular to move to the suburbs. This translated into single-family houses, roomy garages, one and two cars per family and, of course, highways.

Goodbye, trees. Goodbye, open space. Goodbye, downtowns.

Enter: the airline industry. Enter: subsidies. Need a boost, Boeing? We're right here for you. Now, people are starting to move away from suburbs. Now, airports are jammed, despite the cost, the remote locations, the security issues. Government subsidizes airports and highways. Railroads pay for their own infrastructure.

Today for the most part we can't build highways fast enough to hold all the cars. This same phenomenon occurs when you move into a new house. With more rooms, you spread out. Then you get more stuff and you run out of rooms again. So you build add-ons, rent a storage unit, fill up the garage, leave the car outside.

But here's the thing: Despite the hype of the highway and the lure of the jet, people still love to take trains, no matter the cost, the inconvenience, the time. No matter how hard the folks in charge try to shortchange, underfund, undermine their base, people still buy train tickets. No matter how much Amtrak, a corny portmanteau of two words – "America" and "track" – struggles with its ornery heating and air system (should we turn the cars into a terrarium or the Arctic Circle?), we still keep coming back. For some people living far away from airports, trains (and cars) are their only option for getting anywhere. They find their way to itty-bitty stations in the middle of nowhere at all hours of the day and night. They step up on that bright yellow step stool, hand over their luggage to a conductor and enter the train car. They navigate their way to a seat in coach or a sleeper car while the train starts moving to its next stop.

If the intended city doesn't have a train station, Amtrak has instituted, from my experience, a very reliable bus connection system as part of the ticket. If you're headed for St. Petersburg, Florida, whose passenger depot was discontinued February 1, 1984, you detrain in Tampa's historic depot, which dates to 1912. Then you board an Amtrak-contracted bus to a designated bus station in St. Petersburg. The bus waits for the train to arrive; it will not leave without ticketed connecting passengers.

When I wanted to take the train from Phoenix to San Antonio, I waited in a creepy deserted mall parking lot that looked like a set for a zombie movie to catch a van appropriately called the Stagecoach. The only people I saw were some homeless kids on bicycles tending to their phones in a public charging station. The van brought me through the desert to Maricopa, a farm town some forty-five minutes away, the former home of politician Sarah Palin's daughter, Bristol, where the Sunset Limited stops three days a week at 3 a.m. I was happy for the connection (if not the departure time), but for a city the size of Phoenix – the sixth largest city in the country and about to pass Philadelphia – not to have Amtrak service is crazy.

Even people who don't take trains grow misty-eyed at the sound of the whistle, even if the train pulls through their neighborhood in the middle of the night or if it's carrying flammable explosives, toxic waste or kaolin (as it does in Savannah), and drivers have to wait fifteen minutes in their car for the train to snake by. The whistle is enough of an aural memory to remind people of their grandfather or uncle working as a welder, a switchman, a diesel mechanic, a lineman or a conductor or the time they rode the train with their grandmother.

If the industry could just get more money, more respect.

We thought we had a chance when Joe Biden was in office. For forty-four years the former Vice-President and Congressman rode the train roughly 8,000 times, back and forth between Washington, D.C. and his home in Wilmington, Delaware. Surely, the man known as "Amtrak Joe" could have squeezed some money out of Congress. He couldn't. The only hint we got of Joe in the past year was a poster of his new book, *Promise Me, Dad*, a memoir about his son's fight with brain cancer, his family and his time in office. Some employee tacked the cover on the wall of the snack bar of the Capitol Limited. Amtrak employees love Joe.

Granted, Amtrak is trying to sharpen its game. Now you can go online and track the whereabouts of your train in real time. Plus, the quasi-governmental company puts out a ton of statistics on the promising side. On any given day, 300 trains run between 46 states, a far cry from the 2,000 that ran at the turn of the century. Here's what Amtrak doesn't tell you: South Dakota and Wyoming have no service at all. Aside from Phoenix, neither do three other pretty good-sized cities: Louisville (population 760,000), Nashville (685,000) and Las Vegas (584,000). Cincinnati, a town with a metropolitan population of two million, gets a train three times a week. That sounds good until you check closer; they all arrive in the middle of the night.

The following number explains why trains are so often late: Freight trains own ninety-five percent of the tracks traveled by Amtrak passengers.

It comes as no surprise that of the six busiest trains, four run along the Northeast corridor: Washington D.C., Philadelphia, New York and Boston. Chicago and Los Angeles are next. Those six account for forty percent of all tickets sold.

I take the train because highway driving is boring. Drivers tailgate. They pass on the right, hang out on the left. They're rude. I hate adding to the congestion when there's an alternative way to get somewhere. Flying is boring, too. I feel like a second-class citizen, boarding with the hoi polloi. It's a hustle. Airport parking lots are boring, too, and they're expensive.

Trains are never boring. They're irritating, vexing, annoying. They're too hot, too cold, too late or sometimes too early. When the Sunset Limited Maricopa-to-San Antonio train pulled into the south-central Texas town three hours early, at 4 a.m. – it happened to be a light freight day, I was told – you're stuck.

Plus, heading through small-town America and looking out the window at all the trash is disturbing, all the plastic containers, glass bottles, discarded tires, metal shopping carts, dismantled bicycles, abandoned cars, leaning houses, Big Gulp Styrofoam cups, plastic buckets, six-pack beer boxes. Not pretty.

My fellow passengers can be irritating, too. On one twenty-two-hour ride between Dallas and Chicago, I sat two seats back, on the opposite side, of a woman and her two young kids. I get it. She was overwhelmed, impatient, short tempered. Still, it didn't take long to pick up on the only two commands she uttered to her children: "Go to sleep" and "Shut up." I won't lie. I was wishing for the same two actions myself. All I could think about was the W.C. Fields' line: "Go away, kid. Ya' bother me." I caught up with the irksome threesome again in the Chicago station long enough to hear the younger child, maybe three, return his mother's admonishment when she started yelling at him.

"Shut up, mama." Same words, same intonation, same enunciation.

That was hard to hear.

Yes, trains can be late (or early). That can be irritating. No one takes a train if he or she is on a tight schedule. But the people who work at the stations are pretty upfront with expected arrival times. They don't sugarcoat the facts.

People take the train for a variety of reasons. They don't like to fly. They can haul more stuff without additional charges. They can travel with their little kids or grandkids without breaking the bank. Maybe it's easier to get to the train station than the airport. Maybe they lived in Europe where trains are more common and they know from experience how much more of the country they can see from a roomy seat in a car than a cramped seat above the clouds on a plane or trapped in lanes of traffic.

You get to talk to people. When's the last time anyone had a conversation with a stranger in an airport?

Just when I thought I had heard all the reasons for taking the train, I shared a dinner table with a man somewhere in the Midwest. He was returning from San Jose, California, to take care of his mother. She had just had a small stroke, he said. He could have flown. He's not afraid of flying. He had the money for the ticket. He was a house painter with steady work. But he didn't have a driver's license and you need one to get on a plane.

He said his name is Billy the Kid.

He told me you don't need a driver's license on a train. "A birth certificate and/or a social security card will do the trick."

He lost his license a few months ago.

"A cop confiscated my license when I was stopped for resembling someone who had just broken into a house. I was never charged, but as it turns out my license was expired and I never bothered getting another one."

He went on: "I sprung for a sleeper because I'm hauling all my stuff back east and it felt safer that way. But the space feels like a phone booth. The worst thing of all? The door rattles. But I knew that. That's why I always travel with a piece of cardboard, to slip under the door."

I took a sleeper once when I was on a long-distance train to Los Angeles. I didn't like the tiny room. I felt claustrophobic. I felt as if I might be in a tomb.

I lay flat out on my back with the ceiling inches away from my head as if I were undergoing an MRI scan.

The price of a sleeper included three meals. But for my tastes the menu wasn't varied enough. You can end up eating too much. I didn't like the porter sticking his head in my compartment in what felt like every ten minutes asking if I was OK, either.

By now, it's become predictable. I bring up trains in a conversation and wait for the criticism, the grimace, the raised eyebrow. The complaint is not far behind. They're slow!

That's when I say, "I wish they were *slower*." Then I could linger on the details, the streets, the signs, the bridges, the rivers, the mountain of rock, the human element. That's when I ask, "What's your hurry, anyway?"

I mean it, too. I look out the window and I feel frustrated. I want to look a little longer at what's ahead of me, what's next to me, what's passing by. But I can't. Seventy-nine miles an hour may seem sluggish but to me it's fast. Either that or I'm sitting on the wrong side of the car. Near the Great Pee Dee River in South Carolina, the Silver Star passes what looks to be hundreds of flattened cars heaped on top of one another, stacked like pancakes. I'm sitting in the lounge car with one other person sometime in late afternoon. We both see the squashed cars at the same time. Our eyes meet. "What the heck is that?" I say. My fellow passenger has already pulled it up on Google Earth. We are looking down on a car graveyard. I want to be out there talking to the workers. I want to know more. Stop the train!

I'm still kicking myself for what I missed on that Sunset Limited trip to San Antonio. Somewhere near Alpine, home of Big Bend National Park, and Valentine, Texas, in the middle of the desert, of yucca, creosote bushes and pale green agave plants, we passed a permanently installed sculpture of two large framed windows displaying actual Prada shoes and handbags. It was a statement, some say, on consumerism and gentrification. And I missed it. I was either looking out the other side of the train, reading, sleeping or practicing French on my phone.

Sometimes, when I get home, I look back at the photographs from my trips and ask myself what was so compelling that I had to take them. Most of what I see in my photo queue are people. There's that grinning fellow in the Savannah station. He's got an open, happy face with gray whiskers. He's wearing a black hat with Sugar Ray Robinson printed in white on the bill. Then there's the trim, stylish woman who once sat across from me on the Capitol Limited. She's wearing tall leather boots and a suede purple skirt. An open laptop sits on her knees. Why is she there? She looks like an airplane person. Or is that profiling? In the Chicago station I see a trim, tall man in sneakers, short socks down rolled down around his ankles and a sleeveless vest. His legs are crossed; he's reading a paperback. The elderly man in that beautiful Charlottesville, Virginia, station has been sitting on a simple wooden bench for hours. He has a trim beard and is wearing a black cap. His large hands, a gold wedding ring nestled between his knuckles, rest on a walker that doubles as a luggage cart.

I realize it is more fun being in the moment than trying to fit that moment into some meaning. Trains are good for finding the moments.

FORWARD

TAKE TIME TO TAKE STOCK

O N ANY GIVEN DAY, people can throw out a million reasons not to take the train. I've heard them all. They don't have time. Trains are late. How would I get to the station? Some don't believe passenger trains still run. But they're intrigued. They're drawn to the romance. They've watched Alfred Hitchcock's *North by Northwest*. They've seen several versions of Agatha Christie's *Murder on the Orient Express*. They know Jim Jarmusch's *Mystery Train*.

In my hometown of Savannah, people know I like to take trains and to write about trains. They feel comfortable sidling up to me at a concert or in line at the grocery store and saying, "I love your train stories."

The love is strong. Somewhere in their DNA, they "know" trains, especially when they hear Willie Nelson or Arlo Guthrie sing Steve Goodman's song: "Good morning, America. How are you? Hey, don't you know me? I'm your native son. I'm the train they call, 'The City of New Orleans.' I'll be gone 500 miles when the day is done."

But not too many *take* the train. As one confessed, "I'd rather read about you going than myself."

I dedicate this book – *So What's the Hurry, Tales From the Train* – to this person and to others who have not yet bought a ticket and jumped aboard.

Trains take getting used to. They're not cookie-cutter corporate. When the train pulls in to the station you crowd around a car on the tracks and try to find some order. There's no gold, silver or bronze status. An attendant holding a stubby yellow pencil will ask where you are headed. Then he or she will verbally assign you a seat number and mark it on a chart tucked under their arm. Later, after the train starts rolling, the attendant will come by and slip a piece of hand-written scrap paper above your seat with the initials of your final destination (PIT, SAV, NYC).

No one will say, "We're honored to have you fly with us" or, "Thank you for sharing your journey with us." I heard both on a recent flight.

The system on a train is loose. It's analog. It's human. And that is what this book is about, the human aspect – not steam engines, pistons, wheels, rods, diesel, electric conducting rails, monorails, high speed rails, inner city rails, rolling stock or switching yards.

Foamers, stay away. This book is not for you. Foamers is a widely accepted and sometimes pejorative term for railway fans who have gone over the top, who come close to foaming at the mouth when they see a train. I love taking the train; I am not a foamer.

And while there is a lot to be said about the politics or the economics of train travel, it will not come from me. For that I recommend James McCommons' *Waiting On a Train, The Embattled Future of Passenger Rail Service.*

This is a different read. *So What's The Hurry? Tales From the Train* is a book for ordinary, garden-variety people who like to travel but are not racing to see how fast they can get somewhere. Part travelogue, part memoir, part adventure, it's for people who want to take time to take stock, for people who don't mind passing ballfields, wind turbines, patches of creamy white snow, fields of yellow forsythia and fading red barns.

P.S. The City of New Orleans still runs. The Number 58 makes 17 stops between New Orleans and Chicago. It leaves New Orleans Union Passenger Terminal at 1:45 p.m. and after heading through four states, Louisiana, Mississippi, Tennessee, Illinois, it pulls into Chicago's Union Station at 9:15 a.m.

For my ride on the City of New Orleans, I walked into Rouses Supermarket in the French Quarter, a locally owned fine foods store, thinking I might stock up on some provisions, maybe buy a little jambalaya or crawfish etouffee. Instead I found a jar of pomegranate seeds. Perfect snack food.

This is a book for people who get a kick out of learning the little things. Take Amtrak's thrice-weekly Cardinal Line that runs from Washington, D.C. to Chicago. This most scenic route was named for the state bird of the six states it travels through, Illinois, Indiana, North Carolina, Ohio, Virginia and West

Virginia. This book is a close-up, personal look at an America you can't see from a plane high above clouds or from a car sunk in eight lanes of traffic. Highways do not go through small towns; trains do.

If you're deliberate or lucky on your travels, you'll get to stop at some grand old terminals that will never again be built with so much ornamentation, care or embellishment. As you wait for your next train at the 30th Street Station in Philadelphia, you sit under 95-foot-tall ceilings decorated with Art Deco chandeliers. The waiting room is two football fields long.

While Penn Station handles Amtrak's routes to and from New York City, it's worth a visit to the Beaux Arts-designed Grand Central Terminal on East 42nd street, if just to stand under the constellation mural stretched across its green arched ceiling. These days Grand Central handles New York's Metro North lines, subways and buses.

Best case scenario for the future of passenger trains? It's probably not good – unless we start thinking big again. We need to put people to work, thousands of people, to lay more track so we can have more train lines. We need freight companies, who own most of the tracks, and the lowly passenger services, to make peace and operate in harmony. For starters, we need to restore the southern part of the thrice weekly Sunset Limited that used to run between New Orleans and Florida before Hurricane Katrina wiped out the track. Tragically, it never got rebuilt. Presently the Sunset Limited runs between Los Angeles and New Orleans, where it stops.

Amtrak is on fragile funding ground. It doesn't have to be that way. Even with the diminution of travel opportunities people still wait in the dark in the wee hours of the morning looking for that proverbial, "Midnight Train to Georgia." Jump on board. It might be just the ticket you're looking for.

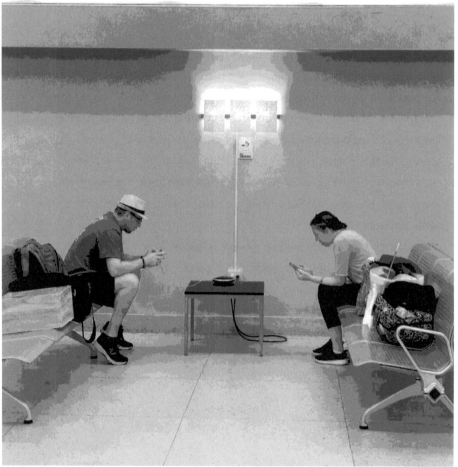

CHAPTER ONE

SLOW AND STEADY

A **FEW YEARS AGO,** flying to Australia, I had what I believe to be my first intimation of death. The first inkling. Nothing suspicious had happened. No trouble with the wings. No fire in the engine. No turbulence. Nothing untoward (unless you choose to dwell on the pending eighteen hours in the air). Yet I had the thought: "I could die right now," followed by, "and that's OK. I've had a good life. None of it ends well. For anyone."

I'm not afraid of those thoughts. I laugh at them. They're true.

On the other hand, I'm not so fond of phrases like "pre-deceased" and "disposition of money." It upsets me such a beautiful word as "will" should be mixed up with matters of death, codicils and enforceable unsecured debts. Before the trip I'd been talking about my will with an attorney. I want to be done with it already. But he's so careful, so cautious. There's always another question. Sometimes my eyes tear up when he's explaining something and I think, I'm glad we're talking on the phone. It's starting to get important.

I'm not afraid to fly. Since I stopped "clocking" in and out for work, I'm just not in that big of a hurry. Maybe that's why I started taking trains. If I knew to whom I could address this appeal I would ask – no, I would beg – "Can you please slow it down a little? I mean, the rest of my life? Can you please make it last just a little longer?"

It's different but not that much different when, tongue firmly in cheek, I politely ask a young mother, "Could you please bonsai your child? Could you please bonsai Baker?" I know she'll be interesting at ten or fifteen, but can't we keep her at six for just a little longer?

I'm not afraid to fly. It's the culture I don't like, the veneer, the gloss, the hustle. Hurry up and wait. Get ready to board but not before people who carry a higher status. Miss your flight? Too bad, so sorry. Oh, we didn't assign you a seat even though you bought a ticket? Sorry. That happens sometimes. The good news is there's another flight in a few hours; maybe there will be an available seat.

That's not the culture of trains.

Last summer, on my way to an early evening departure from Savannah to New York, on the slow but steady Silver Meteor, I pass farmer Robert Johnson on Louisville Road. He is selling watermelons. They were stacked three-deep in the bed of his old Dodge pickup truck piled up high like so many bowling balls, like site-specific sculpture. But unlike bowling balls, no two melons look alike. A few months earlier, in another season, a mess of leafy collards would sit in the truck. One year Mr. Johnson named me queen of his Collard Green Festival on the Port Wentworth, Georgia, property he calls the Promised Land. I was honored. My friend Cara helped me make a boa of collard leaves to wear around my neck. It was a hit. People wanted to eat my collards.

Most days, a friend of Mr. Johnson's sits next to him on the truck's tailgate, their legs swinging in sync. They're facing a cast iron pot of steaming boiled peanuts. Boiled peanuts are an acquired taste in the South and I like them, so I bought a bag to take on the train.

The men are old friends. They are not in a hurry. They're both veterans of the Vietnam War. They congregate regularly in their trucks in front of a modest white concrete building on Louisville Road. In its day, this slightly diagonal road was an important stagecoach route, when Louisville, named for King Louis XVI, was the capital of Georgia.

Their meeting place, on the edge of Savannah's version of a warehouse/ light industrial area, is four traffic lights away from the city's hyped historic downtown district. It might as well be forty miles away.

The train station is minutes from where Mr. Johnson and his friend sit, about twenty minutes from my home if I catch all the lights and don't get behind a phalanx of bicyclists. I drive west on 37th street, north on Martin Luther King Jr. Boulevard and west on Gwinnett Street. I pass the KFC and the Thankful Baptist Church. Then I curve around West Boundary Street, past my purloined urban folk garden, before I turn left on Louisville Road.

That's where I pass the red brick viaduct from 1853. Built by the Central of Georgia Railway, it's an arched beauty that predates the Civil War. It spans West Boundary Street and the Savannah-Ogeechee Canal. A little farther on I pass a few modest white churches to the south and a hill to the north. The hill appeared when I-16 was built. On Sundays my friend Jamie, an ordained Episcopal minister, conducts an outdoor church service for the homeless near a clearing in the woods, which they have set up as their home.

At the railroad station, I pull into a small parking lot. Parking is free. The lot is never full. A smell of disinfectant hits me when I walk through the ample waiting room. I've never seen it crowded. There's a television set high up in one corner; the sound is low. There's one vending machine, four gumball machines and a handful of people sitting next to their luggage, waiting for their train to make its way, one headed for Miami, the other New York City, with stops in between. The station is closed from one-thirty to four every afternoon.

The design of Savannah's current train depot will never make the list of Amtrak's "Great American Stations," a project Amtrak started in 2006 to draw attention to maintaining or redeveloping some really fine terminals. There's no Spanish Renaissance or Elizabethan Revival architecture here, despite Savannah's legacy of fine buildings. There are no Art Deco Grand Halls or stately Beaux Arts columns. It's just a large, one-story, blond-brick building that could be a medical complex in any strip mall in America. It was built in 1962 after misguided city leaders, following some silly trend toward modernism, tore down what's referred to as the old Union Station. That magnificent Beaux Arts building, built between 1899 and 1901 with separate waiting rooms and lavatories for white and black patrons, featured twin onion-domed towers, iron gates, terrazzo floors, Doric frieze and round arched windows. It sat on Martin Luther King, Jr. Boulevard, then called West Broad Street.

By the end of the '50s, the station was considered out of date. In 1961, the State Highway Department purchased the property to make room for Interstate 16 to enter Savannah. The subsequent flyover barreled through what was once a healthy, middle-class African-American neighborhood.

The only visible reference to the station's glory is a painted mural on the side of a Burger King, where the old station sat.

Inside the bland current terminal that could be anywhere in America – forget that it's in a hyper historically conscious city – there are no photos of the old Union Station, no images of the horse-drawn wagons or streetcars that delivered travelers to the terminal. There's no hint of the historic link between the railroad, Savannah's cotton and pine sap (naval) industries and the rest of the country. There's no mention of the transport of troops in the War of 1898, which included Teddy Roosevelt and his famous Rough Riders coming through Savannah, no photos of the black entertainers who came by the dozens. Where's the institutional memory?

Back then, the terminal was an important mode of transportation for African-Americans, although they were still confined to a certain car.

For my first trip to New York City, 829 miles away, I boarded the train in early evening, arriving the next morning smack in the middle of Manhattan.

Now I prefer to travel by day. It's a front-row seat into people's lives.

In Kingstree, South Carolina (seventy-five percent black and the hometown of late R&B singer Teddy Pendergrass), the train stops in the middle of an intersection for passengers to detrain and to board. The conductor stands on West Main Street not far from the Kingstree Christian Bookstore, KP Nails and Spa, Drucker's Drugs and a medical supply house. He raises his hand and stops traffic, such as it is in a town with 3,300 people. Through my window, I turn and watch family and friends give a final hug, a last pat on the back to those they are dropping off. Not far from town, before we pick up speed, we crawl past Joe's Barber Shop, the Lake City Senior Center, signs for skydiving and a line of tanker cars.

Then I see a long, two-story red-brick building. I count ten windows stretching across the second floor. Each window is curved at the top. Above the windows, in capital letters, I read IMPERIAL TOBACCO CO., (OF GREAT BRITAIN AND IRELAND).

My seatmate, about to get off, noticed me looking back at the building. "Tobacco leaves were stored there," he said. "My granddaddy used to work the night shift, get home sometime in the early morning. It sat empty for a long time. They're trying to do something with it now, some community thing."

He didn't sound encouraged.

Before the train could pull away a young man carrying a briefcase, a cell-phone and a stack of papers took the seat next to me. He told me he's a teaching assistant in astronomy. He had traveled south to meet his girlfriend's family. It went well, he said. But now he had four hundred quizzes to grade.

"Two hundred more to go," he announced. He did the first half on the way down. He doesn't have a car; the train was the cheapest way to travel. I glanced over my shoulder and couldn't help but notice students don't sign papers with names anymore. They use numbers.

At the speed we're going, if I squint the graffiti scrawled on stone walls, train cars and overpasses looks like computer animation or images on a flip chart. On a sunny day when the light shines through the trees there's a strobe-like effect that makes reading a book difficult. For those periods, I have a new habit. I've been trying to memorize short poems. I'm trying to fill up the holes that I'm afraid are starting to develop in my mind. I might even go for longer poems, maybe William Butler Yeats' *The Second Coming*. That's the one where he says, "Things fall apart; the centre cannot hold;/ Mere anarchy is loosed upon the world." I think about that line a lot. I might as well commit it to memory.

I've started working with numbers, too. They've been giving me a devil of a time the last few years. Adding and subtracting in my checkbook, remembering what I paid for some of my property taxes. I've gotten too dependent on "look-ing it up."

"Quiz me," I say to Cara, when we're on a trip together. "Ask me the number of our flight. Not right now but in a few minutes."

This has to be good.

Sunday is a busy day on the train. The seats fill up fast.

If I can't read, I lean back and look out the window. It's as relaxing as sitting in the backyard and watching the chickens traipse around, hunting for insects. We pass more water towers, cell towers, tanks, trailers, rows of tractors and telephone poles. Another river. Miles and miles of trees. On one of my first trips I wondered if the day would ever end. Then it dawned on me: It was June 21, the longest day of the year, the summer solstice. I felt better knowing that.

The Silver Service, which runs between New York City and Miami, is crowded. It's not Amtrak's finest line. The cars are old. The tracks are old. The southbound Silver Star no longer has a dining car, prompting some people to call it the Silver Starvation. I didn't have such standards or opinions when I started taking it. Part Luddite, part stubborn, I didn't care how long the trip took. I didn't care if there was no connectivity, no Wi-Fi, no service in a community dining room, no observation car, a.k.a. sightseer lounge with curved floor-to-ceiling windows. I didn't care if we had to wait a half-hour or more for some freight train to pass, if we had to stop so the engineer could climb under the car with a giant wrench and replace a busted air hose ("It's a work of art," one told me once). I did not know, nor did I care about the Silver Service's thirty-nine percent on-time arrival figure.

By now I've been on some better trains, like the one I took across Canada from Vancouver to Toronto, or the electric train in Spain, but I still don't care.

I am old-fashioned. I like the hissing sound of brakes, the screeching of cars coupling and decoupling. I especially like the word "coupling."

I like opening my eyes at night and being surprised by a large and well-lit neon "Jesus is Lord" sign.

From the beginning, I was an Amtrak stoic in the making. Give me a book, some drinking water, a flask of something stronger, a sweatshirt with a hoodie, and I am happy. On Amtrak, it's a slow and steady ride with a few moments of excitement thrown in, just the way I want the rest of my life to be. Is that too much to ask?

CHAPTER TWO
WALK LIKE A PENGUIN

IF YOU'RE GOING TO TRAVEL COACH on Amtrak, sleeping upright, talking to strangers, crossing the country, it helps to go with some good-looking nails. The morning before I departed on the 7:30 a.m. Silver Meteor bound for Chicago, then the Southwest Chief to Los Angeles, I got a mani-pedi, deep blue digits.

For the money, pedicures are the best. The massage chair is a "come with." Sometimes I'm in the mood for all that jostling, sometimes I'm not. The lower leg massage by the one male Vietnamese practitioner at my salon – who adopted the American name Frank before moving here – was another "come with."

Thanks to actress Tippi Hedren, there are Vietnamese salons everywhere. Hedren is the animal rights activist and actress now in her late eighties. She's best known for *The Birds*, Alfred Hitchcock's 1963 horror-thriller movie. Somehow this Hollywood starlet, born in Minnesota in 1930, happened to visit a Vietnamese refugee camp in California. When her long, polished nails dazzled the women (and men), she acted. She flew in her own personal manicurist to pass along the trade. It stuck.

That first night on the three-and-a-half-day trip to California, I scrunch down in my aisle seat, squeezing between my seat-mate – a stranger whose rock-and-roll music was bleeding through her headset – and the inflexible arm rest. I try to form a perfect ball so I can sleep, except my body was anything but a perfect ball. All I could think about was the massage chair of the day before.

Like the chair, the train pulsed. It vibrated. It kneaded. It bucked. I'm a dog on a bed, circling round and round, trying to get comfortable.

Except for one thing: I see I'm going to like this.

I'm happy on a train. From day one, I liked how the conductor stands in front of the door to the car and we all crowd around in no particular order. He or she checks everyone in, talks to each person individually ("Where you going?"), before checking the seat number on a chart secured to a clipboard. No platinum. No gold. No silver-plated. No zones.

"Washington? Three cars that way."

All that before extending a hand to help you up. Later on, a train attendant will come along and look at your ticket. There's a certain amount of trust in that.

The train pulls away from the station by degrees, shyly. In the beginning, the ride is gentle but the tracks in the South are rickety, the tracks are old so there's a certain amount of jostling. By law most trains on most routes can't go faster than seventy-nine miles an hour.

"You wouldn't want them to go any faster," an Amtrak employee told me once when I complained about how slowly we were moving. But now I like the pace. Although train rides are gentle they are also erratic. They dart. They pitch. On this, the first of two dozen train trips I'll take over a six-year period, I don't think I can sleep. I haven't yet mastered the beast. But I have high hopes. I sense we have a future, me and trains.

Nearly two hours later, by the time we get to Charleston, I get up my nerve to walk around. I make a note to myself: Next time you leave Savannah for Charleston, for the annual Spoleto Festival in May, take the train. Forget driving on Highway 17, forget Interstate 95.

I'm unsteady on my feet as I lurch to the bathroom to brush my teeth. I keep my legs wide like a penguin for balance, like the conductor told us. I glance around for ideas of ways to sprawl, perchance to sleep. No two passengers look alike. There is no vanity in riding coach, no privacy. People slouch at all angles. They sag. They snore. They drool.

When I return to my seat, I close my eyes but am convinced I will never sleep. I wonder if train travel is such a good idea after all.

By the time I make my third excursion on the rails, I can fall asleep on a dime. It's become my home. It's my comfort zone. Not as much as before when cell service was spotty and there was no Wi-Fi, when I had to be quick and ready to try to get a signal – a bar or two – as we pulled into a station.

I might have been less addicted back then to connection, to news, to texting.

I yearn for those days. I wish there were a twelve-step program to disconnect, to disengage. There probably is. I'm probably not ready.

But now I've learned to turn the whole connectivity thing off: the messages, the emails, the time, the camera, the news, the calendar. I've learned to shift down in my seat, stretch my sweatshirt hoodie as far as it will go to block a blast of air conditioning on my neck, cover my eyes with a sleep mask. I carry a mini-flask of bourbon, just in case I need a nip. I hardly ever take that nip. The thin, silver flask makes me feel adult. It's my security blanket.

Somehow, I finally do sleep on that first trip. I know this because when I open my eyes it's to daylight, to a thin strip of dark clouds on the horizon, to morning. Best of all, I awake to the aroma of coffee. Someone walking down the aisle past my seat had beat me to the lounge car. When I catch that smell I say, "Hallelujah, thank you, Jesus." Every time. An hour later, when the dining car opens, I do the penguin walk again. I push the button on the four or five pneumatically controlled sets of doors between the cars and feel a gush of outside air. This wakes me up before the coffee. Several cars later I reach my destination: a room of white-covered tables and a lovely woman named Jeannine who seats me community-style at a four-top. I'm sitting with three strangers. We have nothing in common except this one thing: the train.

No one knows me. I can make up any story I wish, any name. I could even pretend I don't speak English. But I don't. Usually I am the one to start talking. One man of indeterminate age – forty? fifty? – who was afraid of flying said he was going to visit his mother. He hadn't seen her in ten years.

"I don't know why it took me so long," he said, playing with his fork. "I was just too busy with my own life."

He was afraid of what he might find, he admitted. "But then she sent me the money for the ticket, so I didn't have a choice."

Another man, hefty, his belly hanging over his belt, was meeting his son and fifty others for a Trans-Am Bandit Run celebrating the fortieth anniversary of *Smoky and the Bandit*. They planned to drive their Trans-Am from Texarkana to Atlanta. A third person did not offer anything about herself.

My contribution to the conversation? "I lost my earring last night."

The Trans-Am guy could relate: "I lost my hearing aide."

I wasn't hearing so well myself. When he complimented me on my woolen skull cap that says, "Skoal" and then asked if I chew, I thought he said, "Are you a Jew?" We got that cleared up right away.

On other trips, I would meet and talk to some Amish people. The Amish don't fly. They don't drive (unless it's in someone else's car). They don't use electricity in their own homes. They always travel in groups. "But we're just people," the woman said.

She spoke English tinged with a form of Pennsylvania Dutch, peculiar to her clan. She and ten other people from their community were heading to a clinic in Juarez, Mexico. One of the children had cancer.

"And the rest of us need a tune-up too," said a black-vested man.

They had been to this clinic before. They trusted the doctor. The children, exact miniature versions of their parents, from their clothes to their crudely cut hair to their pale complexion, go to school until the eighth grade. After that they go to work. They speak their language to maintain the tradition.

"Guess how many children I have?" The woman, her face scrubbed so clean it looked pink, as if she were blushing, asked me out of the blue.

Answer: ten plus 78 grandchildren and twelve great-grandchildren.

She didn't ask how many I have. How would it have sounded to say, "None," although I do claim two by a close connection with a friend. I'm glad she didn't ask.

This particular group was dressed in indigo-blue pants, skirts and blouses. Some women wore stiff white caps tied under the chin. White means married. Black means unmarried. But no one wears colors. Never colors. They don't like to draw attention to themselves, they say. When I hear that I say nothing. They can't help but stand out. Don't they know they stand out? The men have long beards, no mustaches. They wear long white shirts without collars, lapels or pockets. The shirts remind me of the Nehru jackets of the Seventies.

Even in their seats at night they sleep politely. They look neat. The men sit straight in their chairs, feet on the ground, the women hold the children in their laps.

I ask about another group of Amish who were dressed slightly differently. "They are higher up," a man offered. He seemed reluctant to elaborate. When I push, he broke down and said, almost in a whisper, "They have phones. In their garages." Another young man who spoke their language wore a purple plastic bracelet, jeans and sneakers. His hair was layered. No bowl cut for him. No black and white, either. I asked him why he wasn't dressed the same way. He said he hadn't decided to join the church even though he still lived at home and was twenty-five. He has a phone. He has a car.

He talked to me but without curiosity, without affect. His eyes looked down.

They reminded me of certain sects of Hasidic Jews, outsiders, self-contained, reluctant to mix with the regular people. They – the Amish – work hard to remain in the minority. Or maybe it's in their nature. They're very obedient.

When we stopped in Albuquerque the conductor announced, "We leave in twenty minutes. If you don't get back in time, there's a hotel two blocks to the right and up a hill. Fourteen dollars a night. You can pick up the train tomorrow."

He wasn't hostile or sarcastic in offering that information. Just matter of fact. The conductor did not follow any script.

Anyway, what's the hurry? It's not like when you're six and you want to be ten ("please dear God, let me be ten") so you could be in double digit numbers. Ten sounded good. Sixteen sounded good, too, when I was twelve. Then I could get a license. Then I could drive. When I was twenty, I wanted to be twenty-eight. Then I could say I was in my late twenties. I thought that had a nice ring to it.

Now I'm seventy-five and guess what? I do not want to be 78 or 83. That does not have a nice ring. At least now I know I won't be getting early onset Alzheimer's. Cross that off the worry-list.

Not that I don't face those moments. I just wish I could wear a button that reads, "I don't remember names." Where you live? Yes. What you do? For sure. But no names. I even know what to say when people ask if I'm retired. "Writers never retire," I say. These days I have to take out my phone, start at the "A's" and go through every contact if I'm looking for someone's name and I can't remember it. It was working just fine until I saw the movie *Still Alice*. Alice, played by Julianne Moore, is a linguistics professor who can't seem to find the words or the keys or the phone or the book she's reading. Spoiler alert: the movie does not end well. And she was a linguist. She was an intellectual.

Now, when I run into someone and I can't remember his or her spouse's name, I find myself saying, "How's your bride?" Or "How's that groom?" If I get the person's name wrong, I say, "You cut your hair," or "Didn't you used to have a beard?" Sometimes it works. I've started to call people "kids." It's gotten a good response. "I like that," said my friend Richard.

This is what I know for sure about age. We all get shorter. Gray hair doesn't curl up as well as brown hair once did. Handwritten thank-you notes go a long way. The cost of duplicating car keys is insane. It's best not to do the math when you find out someone was born after 9/11.

Plus, my fellow seventy-year-olds know what kind of presents to bring a person. For my last birthday, my friend Elaine – maybe a year older, maybe a year younger, who can remember? – brought me a tray of homemade brownies. The recipe came from Katharine Hepburn (born in 1907, died at 96). I had enough brownies to eat for breakfast for a whole week.

Have you ever heard anyone say they want to be seventy-five? No. I am not interested in being any older than I am. This age is just fine, thank you.

And that's why I prefer the train. I'm not interested in getting anywhere fast. Just the opposite. I prefer to slow down the days, to stretch out the weeks and the years. The only way I can think to do that is to take the train. Seventy-nine miles an hour is just fine with me.

I'm right there with the two conductors on my last train who hadn't seen one another in a while.

"How you hanging, my brother?" said the one whose four-day shift was ending. "You staying strong?"

The last time I checked, I was.

CHAPTER THREE

A PIECE OF COCONUT CAKE

FIFTY-THREE YEARS AGO, I went to Europe with a friend. The summer of '65. The summer of Bob Dylan's *Mr. Tambourine Man*. We had a Eurail Pass and a book, *Europe on $5 a Day*.

In my mind Dylan was talking about me when he sang, "I'm not sleepy and there is no place to go to." I was trying to reverse that. In everyone else's mind, my friend and I were a couple of well-behaved, middle-class Jewish girls from the suburbs with the bare bones of an itinerary, no cellphone, no credit card. We had our passports, hard copies of our plane tickets home, a blue book of perforated traveler's checks and copies of those check numbers "just in case they got stolen." No cyber security issues then.

We were open to the world.

I long to be that person again.

Today before I pack for a trip, I think: What if I crack a tooth on an almond or lose a tooth to some popcorn? That is not an attractive look. As a precaution I will soak the almonds first and skip the popcorn. What if I twist my knee again, like I did in Tel Aviv three years ago? I'll bring a knee sleeve, the black one. I'll pack plenty of Advil.

I don't remember bringing any Advil in 1965. Or a knee sleeve.

In January 2016, I bought an Amtrak USA Rail Pass. A little more expensive than the Eurail, a few more rules, a little more confusing about what I could and could not do.

I would travel by myself. Sometimes it's easier that way.

I chose the 30-day option. That allowed me to get on and off the train twelve times. It cost $689. There are also 15-day passes with eight exits for $459 and a 45-day pass with eighteen chances to get on and off the train. That one cost $899. I would start with the Empire Builder that runs across the top of the country, change to the Coast Starlight and then ride the Pacific Surfliner down the coast of California where I would detrain and spend a few days with my transplanted Detroit cousins, Nancy, Bonnie and Marcia. I wasn't sure how I would get back to Savannah. The pass is tricky. Segments get gobbled up fast. You're supposed to book your individual ticket ahead of time. I don't think that's always necessary.

The Empire Builder starts in Chicago and ends in Portland, Oregon. If I stayed on the train the whole way to Portland, that would count as one segment. But I wanted to stop in Minneapolis – and to get to Chicago meant taking the Silver Meteor to Washington, D.C., then the Capitol Limited to Chicago. There go two segments, right out of the box. Ridiculous.

I flew to Chicago.

I wanted to visit someone in Eugene, Oregon. Since the Empire Builder ends in Portland I would have to ride – make that, waste – two more Amtrak segments, to and from Eugene, before reboarding in Portland for my ride down California. I felt boxed in and the trip hadn't even started.

Instead, I bought a round-trip bus ticket between Eugene and Portland.

From Chicago's O'Hare International airport, I took the Blue Line "L" train downtown. Five dollars. I wasn't in a hurry, I reminded myself. This wasn't a race. I could figure things out by myself or I could ask someone. English is my first language. I would piece together public transportation. I read the map and got the Southport "L" to Belmont Avenue, where I would spend the night with my friend, Nicole. The weather was in the single digits. I couldn't remember why I chose January as a time to travel. Nicole and I stayed inside that night, moving from couch to chair to stools in the kitchen, taking the threads of our conversation with us. Until we did the math it felt like the beginning of our friendship, some fifty years earlier.

The next afternoon I took the "L" down to Union Station where I would board the afternoon Empire Builder to St. Paul/Minneapolis. As planned, I would visit a couple of Savannah transplants, Suzanne and Brian. The train pulled in around 10:30 that night. Too late for public transportation and too cold. I Uber-ed from the venerable and refurbished neoclassic Union Depot in St. Paul across town to my friends in Minneapolis.

My first leg of the pass.

Then it got real. If I thought it was chilly in Chicago, it was frigid in Minneapolis.

There were days when neither Suzanne nor Brian would go outside without three pairs of pants, a serious pair of gloves and an adequate hat. The only time Minneapolis public schools close is when the temperature drops below thirty *below*. The weather doesn't stop other activities. I saw people kite skiing in Powderhorn Park. They are tough people, these Minnesotans.

The next day I went for a walk with pajama bottoms under my jeans, three layers on top and my cushy down winter jacket that doubled nicely as a pillow on the train. We went sightseeing along the Mississippi River and saw the refurbished, repurposed Pillsbury, Gold Medal Flour and General Mills buildings. The sun was out. That helped. So did their car. It had heated seats. We went to Magers & Quinn, one of the city's two classic independent bookstores, ate a famous Juicy Lucy hamburger at Matt's Bar. The cheese is melted inside the burger. We drank a beer at the Chatterbox, a quintessential neighborhood bar.

I like Minneapolis. They designed it so every home is within a half mile or six blocks of a park or playground. The city has two hundred thousand trees and a bookstore, the Wild Rumpus, that houses two pet rats, two chinchillas, two ferrets, several fish, three cockatiels, two mourning doves, one tarantula, one African desert lizard (Spike) and four cats.

Trying to be spontaneous, I was still contemplating the rest of my rail route. I couldn't let it rest. Every morning I'd shuffle down the narrow wooden stairs of Suzanne and Brian's rental house, sit at the cozy breakfast table and study the 136-page Amtrak System Timetable. A former Savannah Amtrak agent, due to retire in four months, took a walk on the wild side and smuggled it out to me, slipping it under the glass at the station in Savannah, making sure no one was watching. It's one of those bound timetables printed in small font on newsprint. Yellow arrows point up and down the columns of cities with "Dp" and "Ar" for departing and arrival times.

As I studied the routes, my friends spent their day looking for a house to buy. That was work, too. Minneapolis is so popular, houses get snatched up the minute they go on the market. Frequently, people outbid the asking price.

Hmm. Did I want to get off in Fargo, North Dakota, to see if people like Frances McDormand's character in *Fargo* really do say, "you betcha," "dontchaknow" and "oh yah"? Possibly. Except the train pulls in at 3:34 a.m. Nah. That wouldn't work. That is the beauty and the trouble with trains – they go through the night – but arrival and departure times are not always the most convenient.

Shelby and Glasgow, exotic sounding names, both in Montana? Maybe. Lots of empty spaces. That sounded appealing. But in the winter? Then there was the connectivity issue between stations and towns to consider. Connectivity is a big thing in train travel. Is there a bus to take you to town, to a nearby hotel? Not every city is like Portland, where there are bus and urban trains bridging railway travel and airports. Where do you go when you get into a place at 4 a.m.?

I left Minneapolis without a plan. Brian, because it was sub-zero and he's a nice guy, drove me to the station in his seat-heated car to catch the 10:20 p.m. I arrived early. I had a chance to look around the place.

That's when it hit me. This wasn't the same station I arrived in four years earlier when I visited my cousin Carol. In my haste to find an Uber three days before, I hadn't noticed. The first station must have been temporary while they worked on this $250 million Neo-Classical renovation known as the St. Paul Union Depot. Someone at Amtrak and in Minnesota was thinking big – to restore this historic neoclassical Union beauty from 1926 when there are only two trains a day, south early in the morning, west late at night. That's a far cry from the two hundred eighty-two trains in 1923, when the station was built. Maybe there are more stops on their schedule now. Maybe they have other plans. I'm guessing there will have to be lots of art installations, live performances, graduation parties, wedding receptions, Bar/Bat Mitzvah celebrations, Christmas parties and art shows to make it worthwhile. Suzanne does yoga in the depot and shops at the farmers market. That counts. I'm betting a movie or two has been shot there. There is a ping-pong table. Maybe they could consider a second ping-pong table. They have the room.

During the renovation trains stopped in a much smaller station in an industrial section of Minneapolis. That's where I remember squeezing onto a bench waiting for the Empire Builder to take me home to Savannah. I recall sitting next to a nicely dressed, buttoned-up man of a certain age speaking on the phone. As a journalist I'm a professional eavesdropper, a snoop by nature. The conversation interested me.

"You'll know me," the man said into the phone.

Maybe it's a drug deal, I thought, hoping I was on to something. Maybe he was dressed in a way to throw people off. Someone had just told me I'm the perfect person to drive drugs across the country. Middle-aged. Gray-headed. Appropriate. He could pass, too.

"I'm the only one in the lobby with a tie on," the man said. "It's a bowtie, gold and maroon."

When he hung up I told him I couldn't help but notice his tie and socks as well. Same dual colors. Nice colors. I asked him about it.

"You're not from around here," he said with great insight. "They're the colors of the Golden Gophers from the U of M."

"You're right. I'm not from around here. Where I'm from, U of M stands for the University of Michigan not the University of Minnesota."

He laughed.

It turns out he was the chief investment officer for the University of Minnesota. We got to talking about football. He told me the football coach at his university makes $1.4 million.

"Same with the basketball coach," he said. "The president of the college makes $625,000."

Does everyone but me know this?

Then he explained why. "Branding, it's the main reason for football. That and alumni associations."

I finished his thought.

"Which brings in the money."

He nodded as if to say, "Well, duh."

"I'm here to meet a man I've never met before," he said. "He told me he'll be wearing a flannel checkered shirt. He's coming from Minot, North Dakota to buy my mother's five-year-old Buick. $11,000. She died last month. He saw it on eBay. I've got the key right here in my pocket. He's working for one of the oil companies. There are so many people working out there he couldn't find a used car to buy. The auto supply stores have empty shelves. No one can find plumbers. Or spark plugs. It's hard to find a place to rent, too. Two-hundred-fifty-square-foot apartments are going for $2,000. There's also a serious lack of women."

When the train pulled in, I tried to see the two men as they connected. I wanted to see the handoff, money for key. But I lost my man in the rush.

Four years later, people boarding in the new depot weren't nearly as chatty. It was 10:30 at night. It was dark, cold, and, if not creepy, a little ominous standing in line in that empty, cavernous building that held so much history. The room was chilly. We held our tickets, pulled our suitcases and tried to manage bulky bags and overcoats.

We listened closely as the conductor told us which car to board. We didn't want to stand outside in the cold very long. Once on the train we all settled in pretty quickly for the night. You have to get lucky with the heating situation on Amtrak. It's either very cold or very hot. We caught a hot car. This time around I didn't mind.

I took a nip of Bourbon, scrunched down in the seat, pulled my hat down low and fell asleep easily. If something didn't come up – some wild and woolly idea of where to get off – I would stay on schedule and detrain in Portland.

Is spontaneity more difficult in winter? When you get older and more fearful? Maybe.

I opened my eyes in Rugby, North Dakota, "the geographical center of North America," said the affable car attendant. "Good morning, North Dakota. Can I get a good morning? Folks, the dining car is now open for service."

I peered out the window at the dim light of a dreary February morning. There were no billboards, no cars, a blanket of snow as we pulled into the station.

Conductors have different personalities. Some like to elaborate, others don't. The conductor on this train is a man who seems to enjoy his job. I fish around for my shoes, tuck my toothbrush in my back pocket and head downstairs for a trip to the loo and my first cup of coffee of the day. Long-distance trains are double-decker. Bathrooms, luggage storage (if you're inter-ested), and eating for the elderly and the disabled are on the lower level. So is the snack bar.

About an hour later we get another announcement. We were in Minot, "rhymes with 'why not'," the conductor said.

And then there was Elissa. She appeared in the front of our car, as if out of nowhere. She's a mechanic, dressed in puffy winter gear and wielding a well-worn blow torch wrapped in duct tape. She had a cheerful Midwestern demeanor.

"I'm here to unfreeze your sinks and showers," she said, as if it was some-thing she did every day. "It's the switches. They're all froze up." I look out the window, my default gesture on the train. The red brick Minot bank clock read, "O degrees."

"Might as well make this a smoke stop," the conductor said. "We'll be here awhile."

I made my way through what I call the "smoker's lounge" into Minot's renovated beauty, a station they call the Great Northern Railway Depot. I don't smoke but I identify with the outsider status of those who do. I was one of them in spirit. They are prepared, these diehards, these outliers, unlit cigarettes shook from the pack, dangling from their lips, lighters in hand, as they wait for the doors to open, with or without a winter jacket. They're going to make the most of the stop.

The Minot depot was renovated in 2010 with wooden wainscoting, tile flooring, wooden benches and pressed-tin ceiling. Funds came from the American Recovery and Reinvestment Act, an Obama initiative, a concept in these heady post-Obama days that is already sounding old, maybe nostalgic. Inside the cozy depot, the television news was focused on rioting in Berkeley, California. Some fifteen hundred students were gathering in front of Sproul Hall to protest the appearance of a pro-Trump speaker. Even the news sounded dated.

When we finally pull out I notice a sign for the Western Plains Opera Company. I grab my phone and pull up its website. The company has been around since 1976. Kudos, Minot, North Dakota. Why did I ever doubt you?

Balancing my coffee, I make my way to the double-decker lounge car with the curved windows, the skylight, the views. That's where I see a foursome sitting at a table with a white flaky triple-decker coconut cake placed in the middle. So cheerful. So Midwestern.

"Birthday?" I say, thinking how much I love eating something sweet in the morning with my coffee, especially coconut cake.

"Yep," a congenial man answers with that broad Midwestern accent. "Sixty-fifth. Plus, my twenty-fifth wedding anniversary."

"Where you headed?" I ask.

"Spokane," answers a woman. "We're going to interview my 90-year-old uncle before it's too late. But first we're going to the Izaak Walton Inn in Glacier National Park for a few nights. That's in Montana. Where are you headed?"

"I'm not sure. Somewhere."

We got to talking because that's what you do on a train. Joy, a retired Catholic school principal in Champaign, Illinois, started talking about how she sold worms for a penny apiece as a kid in her father's "men's bar," in upstate New York. Her husband, the birthday boy, is an engineering professor at the University of Illinois. He wrote a grant and set up a teacher science camp with a community college of the Blackfeet Indian reservation near Essex, Montana. They were traveling with their brother-in-law and his wife. She's a nurse. They live in Minot. She and the professor keep up the family farm in Dickinson, North Dakota, which they operate as a cash-rent farm, "mostly wheat and sunflowers (for sunflower oil)." They love to take the train.

Then, Joy reads my mind and says the magic words.

"Would you like a piece of cake?"

CHAPTER FOUR

ELEVENTH HOUR CHANGE OF PLANS

WITH A WHOLE EMPTY DAY looming ahead on a train, one piece of coconut cake, no matter how tasty or flaky, only goes so far. The wholesome foursome from downstate Illinois settle into a game of hearts. They ask me to join, but I'm not a card player. I take my piece of cake, eat it with my coffee and head to the dining car. I need a real breakfast. It turns out to be an eight-dollar plate of scrambled eggs, a couple of sides and more coffee. A white paper cloth covered the table and while it was not ironed, bleached or cotton, it did the job. The cutlery was hard plastic, same as the dishes.

"Grits or potatoes?" the waiter asks.

"Are the grits any good?" I ask back.

"Depends on what you mean by good."

"I'm from Savannah, Georgia," I offer.

"I'm from Jacksonville, Florida," he said. "You better go with the potatoes."

I am seated with a single man more concerned with issuing pronouncements than initiating conversation. He was "mansplaining," slightly interesting but not very interactive.

"Did you know there were sixty million buffalo back in the twentieth century," he said, not looking for an answer. "All killed to feed man's greed and to build railroad tracks. We are really a disgusting people."

He had that right.

I nodded a lot, ate my breakfast, drifted off a little and headed back to my seat. I was rereading Diane Smith's *Letters from Yellowstone*. The subject and location seemed appropriate. And it was short, one of my requirements for books I tuck away for a long trip. I loved it the first time I read it for a college class I once took called Environmental Literature. It was better the second time around. Now I would have the space to consider its meaning without dashing to its end, a problem of mine when it comes to reading.

So what's the hurry? I ask myself, yet again. Settle in. Enjoy the moment. Slow down. That's why you like riding the train, remember? It sounds morbid but the fact is the end will come soon enough. I might as well enjoy the middle part.

The book is a fictional collection of letters (an epistolary novel) about a young, spirited and independent woman in love with botany and adventure. In 1898 she applies through the mail for a job as a naturalist with a group of scientists from Boston who are heading to Yellowstone National Park on a field study. Considering the era, she knows she will never get the job if she uses her real name, Abigail. Instead she applied as A.E. Bartram. That she might be related to the celebrated botanist William Bartram doesn't hurt her chances. It is historic and literary fiction at its best. The author lives in Montana.

I appreciate the synchronicity, although I hadn't planned it. On the connecting train to Minneapolis I started rereading another short book, *In the Lake of the Woods,* by Tim O'Brien. I didn't remember the book takes place in Minnesota.

On my last long train trip a year before on the Southwest Chief between Chicago and Los Angeles, I happened by accident to be reading James McBride's *The Good Lord Bird.* This is a lively bit of historical fiction about a slave who hitches up with a ragtag group of rebels joining abolitionist John Brown to stage a slavery revolt. I bought it in Monterey, California, and finished it when the Capitol Limited, which runs daily between Chicago and Washington, D.C., pulled through the Blue Ridge Mountains. That's where the Shenandoah and Potomac rivers merge into Harper's Ferry, West Virginia. That was the home of the raid.

Trains are great places to read. If the dining car offered more variety – and the bathrooms were better – I could have spent the entire three-week period of my USA Rail pass glued to my seat, hidden from the world, reading, dreaming, slouched over in my low-rent seat in coach, absorbing the country, overhearing conversations, meeting new people with my new anonymous personality. Next time.

I was snug. Someone else was doing the driving. I didn't have to navigate. I didn't have to talk. I didn't have to do anything. I was happy. But that morning after breakfast something nagged at me, a loose thread dangling out front, waiting to be pulled. I started thinking about the Izaak Walton Inn in Glacier National Park. I heard about it from my new friends who gave me the piece of coconut cake. Walton was a writer from the seventeenth century, someone I never read and probably never will.

Still. The seed had been planted. Maybe I should get off there. Maybe that was the spontaneous stop I was seeking. I fished out the Amtrak Timetable Schedule, found the Essex, Montana, stop, squinted my eyes at the small print and followed my finger down the columns of type. We were scheduled to pull in at 8:30 that night. Perfect. I found the inn on my phone, "dialed" them up and made a reservation. I asked and learned a van would pick me up, no problem. I would spend the night – or two if I wanted – in Montana and get back on the train for Oregon.

I was pleased with myself, so I continued on. I checked out hotels in Portland, where I planned on detraining the day after, and made another reservation in a hotel easily reached by a simple ride on the city's Green Line, a light rail. I had never been to the faddish Portland. I had three things I needed to do: go to Powell's Books, eat something from a food truck, buy another phone charger. I had already lost one. Small goals. Portland is a perfect example of how transportation systems should work.

I returned to my book and spent the rest of the day reading, staring out the window, and dozing. I was taking a break from life, from making decisions.

Snow was starting to fall. It was peaceful, but as I walked downstairs for a late afternoon cup of coffee, and maybe something sweet, I found drama.

"Are you with them?" the man tending the snack bar asked. "Because they're finished. Too much drinking." I knew who he was referencing. They had boarded in Minot with wrapped skis and snowboards. Did he really think I was with them? That's cool, I thought.

Just on time, the conductor announced, "If you're caught smoking, the next stop will be your last stop. Amtrak is a family train. No profanity, please."

It turns dark early in February, especially so far north. By the time we got to

Cut Bank, Montana, then Browning, I could make out very little outside the window. But I did know Essex, my stop, was coming up. I knew where I was going, the car conductor did not. The little piece of paper above my seat still read "POR" for Portland. There was no one to remind me of my stop near the Izaak Walton Inn or to tell me where to get off. Amtrak does have a system, no matter how low-tech or casual it may seem, and I had messed with it.

In anticipation of Essex, I hauled my suitcase down from the shelf above, navigated the curvy, narrow stairs and got ready to get off the train. I was the only one there. "Excuse me," I said to a uniformed Amtrak person who happened to be around.

"This is where I get off for Essex, right?"

"No!" he barked, annoyed. "It's two cars back. Quick! Go upstairs, walk down to the end of the next car and then down the stairs. Hurry."

I started to panic. I could hear the brakes squeaking. I could feel the train slowing down. No time to drag my suitcase up the twisting stairs, step by step. I had to pick it up. Bumping wall to wall for balance, as if I were in bumper pool, I made it to the top. Don't fall, I urged. Don't fall. I hurried through the car, past sleeping passengers, through the set of pneumatic doors between cars, then down a narrow flight of circular stairs. I was still standing. The train hadn't stopped yet.

"You weren't supposed to get off here," the next conductor said as he opened the doors to help me down. He was irked. "Hurry up. We're about to leave."

Considering this train has a 72 percent on-time arrival rate, I thought he was taking his job a bit too seriously.

I emerged into darkness, an untended, uncovered, isolated platform enveloped in white. I was in a snow globe. This is what's known as a flag station, though I failed to see any flags. Snow had been falling for hours. About fifty feet up a slight incline I spotted a van with its headlights on. I trudged up the hill, wearing the wrong shoes but not worrying about it. The van door opened. People were in the front so I scooted into the back. That's when I saw my new best friends, the celebrating foursome. They had gotten out at the right place at the right time. They were surprised to see me.

"The place sounded too good to pass up," I said.

"It was the cake, right?" the woman said. "We still have some left."

I took a breath. My heart was racing. I had made it. We drove up the hill and in minutes we were at the lodge, a place that dates back to 1939 when trains, bless their sooty, noisy, segregated, buffalo-killing, analog selves, were still popular, still holding their own, back when the country supported 2,000 passengers a day.

The inn was built for the Great Northern Railway and sits on a secluded piece of property surrounded by forest. There is nothing corporate or cookie-cutter about it. I could stay in a small refurbished caboose a quarter of a mile away, a cabin or the inn. I chose the inn. The clerk warned me: There are no televisions and internet connection is spotty. The restaurant was still open.

In the dining room, a mechanical toy train circles the upper perimeter of the wall. Old train fixtures are retrofitted into light fixtures. There was a pool table, a foosball game and shuffleboard table in the basement. I sat by myself and enjoyed a bowl of butternut squash soup, a double order of beet salad, and the evening special, a rainbow "Ruby red" Idaho trout sautéed with almonds, topped with herbed butter, served with cranberry wild rice.

"And a glass of wine, too, please," I said. "Preferably something that hasn't already been opened."

The cutlery was not plastic.

The waitress, eager for someone to talk to, told me she had gone to the Savannah College of Art and Design, but when she joined her boyfriend at Yellowstone for the summer, she fell in love with the area and got a job at the inn. "It's heaven," she said. "I never gave two thoughts to Montana. I'm from Connecticut. I have no regrets."

After dinner, I headed to the front room. I sunk into a low and soft easy chair in front of a ripping fire in an enormous stone fireplace. The daily newspaper, *The Hungry Horse News*, (from Hungry Horse County) beckoned. I passed it up for now. Before I fell asleep in my chair I trudged upstairs, used a large oversized key to open my door and fell asleep quickly in my room under a heavy, woolen, Western-themed blanket. I was lying flat, in a bed. I thought, I'm so lucky it's dumb. In the morning the sound of the crackling fire, directly below my room, woke me up.

Heaven.

I went down for coffee and sat by the fire. I fully intended to spend the day cross-country skiing. Even though I've gone only once in my life, through the Waveland Golf Course in Chicago some fifty years earlier, I thought it would be the perfect sport. Low-impact, minimal skill, plenty of exercise.

Then someone opened the front door letting in Arctic gusts of air. He must have been staying in one of the caboose cabins. He was garbed in bulky all-weather pants, scarves, gloves, boots, hat. I got up, stepped outside for a second and examined close-up the round, wooden thermometer hanging on the porch. Minus nine degrees. I took a quick survey of the clothes I had in my suitcase – jeans and sneakers – and reconsidered my plans. Yes, I could rent skis and poles. But what about boots? A facemask? Gloves? Pants? Long underwear?

"There's always the hot tub," said Bo, the man behind the desk. He had been watching me. Reading my mind? My face? "We have towels and a robe, too. Let me know if you want to go."

Not a hard choice. I said yes, which meant he had to manually turn on the jets.

"The turn-on button is frozen. You should know we're expecting thirty inches of snow by the end of the day."

Lord have mercy. We are not in Kansas anymore. Or Savannah.

The hot tub sounded much more my speed. I walked out the back door to take a look. Zero degrees out there too. Could I do this? I returned to the front desk, gathered some towels, gathered my courage and headed outside. The walk-way was supposed to be heated to keep the path free of ice. It wasn't. I walked carefully. No falling.

Steam billowed up from the one-hundred-four-degree water. The tub sat under giant spruce and juniper trees surrounded by large rocks, all different shapes, all different colors. Again, I thought: Could I do this? I hadn't bothered putting on a bathing suit. It was too much trouble. It might give me too much time to change my mind. I had the place to myself. I dropped my drawers, held my breath and stepped in, naked.

Look at me, I thought, moving my arms and legs around in the hot water. I did it. I was very pleased with myself. As if on cue, the snow started drifting down. Softly at first, the flakes floating at random, then heavier, thicker. The snow covered my towel. Thirty inches, the clerk had said. He wasn't kidding.

I didn't see my new best friends again. They went shopping. That night, twenty-four hours later, I packed up, crawled back into the van and headed for the flag stop. The Empire Builder was late. The driver and I sat in the heated van for thirty minutes. The radio played.

"How will they know I'm here?" I asked.

"They'll see my lights," the driver said. "And I can read theirs."

A train headed our way. My driver could look down the tracks and see by the number of lights if it was the right train. It wasn't. This one was hauling freight.

As we waited, the snow kept falling. Maybe I should have stayed a few more days. More second-guessing. Too late. The Empire Builder came. The train attendant extended a hand and I took it to step up the platform. Maybe a minute later, no more than that, the train pulled away into the darkness; I found a seat with no one next to it and drifted off. Somewhere around Spokane, the Empire Builder would split. One part headed north to Seattle while my section continued to Portland.

I awoke to the Columbia River running alongside the train, the approaching Mt. Hood in the distance, and the sweet voice of an eight-year-old boy sitting behind me asking his mother, "Are we going through a cave again or it is just dark?" That morning she told me they were traveling from Minot to Seattle. "Much cheaper," she said. "Much cheaper. And I wanted my son to experience the train, while we still have them."

I got some coffee and headed for the observation car, what Amtrak calls the sightseer lounge. We followed the river for what seemed like hours.

All along the ride, a thin layer of snow dusted abandoned cars, the red roofs of train stations and parked Airstream trailers, much the same way the frosting floated over that homemade triple-decker coconut cake from the wholesome Midwest foursome. Tree limbs were covered in ice, part of the river too.

"OK folks, we're coming in on track four. We'll be in Portland in twenty minutes."

Whatever was happening in the rest of the world or wherever the rest of my trip took me, I didn't care. I was on a train. I was happy.

CHAPTER FIVE
THE TUESDAY DISCOUNT

IN THE SPACIOUS SIGHTSEER LOUNGE a few hours from Portland, Oregon, a lanky young man wearing headphones started doing some expansive yoga moves in a showoff-y way. He kind of ticked me off. He wasn't quite a mansplainer like some old white guy, but through his actions he was on his way. He was just taking up too much space. He has his whole life ahead of him. Show a little respect, will you?

I wonder if he's heard of Epley's maneuver, also known as old person's disease. It's when gunk gets stuck in the middle ear and you feel dizzy as you stand up. Probably not. I wonder if he's ever shelled out $6,000 for a dental implant only, a few years later, to sit and hear the dentist tell you the screw of the implant broke. Doubtful. Not yet, at least. I'm quite certain he never thinks of dental problems and hasn't given any thought to the notion that thousands of years ago most people died with their same teeth because they didn't eat so much sugar or processed food. His teeth are still white. He wouldn't know what to say if a dental hygienist offered to pull some errant facial hairs.

"These clear latex gloves can really grip the hairs," the hygienist said, going for a couple dozen on my chin. Why didn't anyone tell me they were there? "Oops! There's another one. Got it."

The yoga youngster's skin is smooth, his hair thick. No age spots. No red blotches. No marks at all. His blood has not started to thin. No restorative yoga for him. Not yet.

I hate him.

Carl Jung says life begins at forty. Everything before that is just research or fact-finding. If this guy is in his research phase, where am I, in this business of life, in the middle of my eighth decade?

Many mornings when I wake up my overarching desire is to get on a train and go somewhere. Anywhere. It doesn't really matter where. Just away. This is not new. When I was in my early twenties, in my first job in Chicago, when I had no friends and no real passion for being a high school English teacher, I'd ride my bike. One Saturday I got on my bike, rode downtown and found myself in the middle of a parade, the "Captive Nations" parade. Huh? Estonia, Latvia, Lithuania. Put me on "Jeopardy." Ask that question: Who lives in Latvia, anyway?

A few months later in winter, also on a Saturday, I climbed the platform on 71st Street and caught the South Shore commuter line to Chicago's old Union Station. I picked a train at random and rode to and from Des Moines, Iowa. I don't remember talking to anyone. Now when I check I can't find a train from Chicago to Des Moines. Maybe I made it up. Maybe it wasn't Des Moines. Maybe the schedule changed when Amtrak took over in 1971. But it was Iowa. I saw cliffs, I saw the Mississippi, I went home happy.

The decades passed. I no longer teach school. Everything was going along swimmingly in my life until New Year's Day a few years ago when I announced in front of a group of friends my resolution for the year: I planned to do one cartwheel a day starting right then. No big deal. A modest goal.

We had rented a house on Tybee Island, near my home in Savannah. Most of the people were decades younger but we got along well enough. When one of them, an art teacher in her late thirties who just put her dog to sleep, said, "I'm going to start marking time by when someone's pet dies," I got the feeling she was beginning to have her own awareness of life. It doesn't go on forever.

My cartwheels were never perfect but I could manage to get one leg over the other. Let's just say I could do a decent cartwheel.

And then on that fateful New Year's Day, I saw I couldn't.

I probably can't rifle a ball from shortstop over to first base, either. Forget jumping rope, which I used to do to improve my vertical jump for volleyball and to get my heart rate up. Not now. Too hard on the knees. Too risky. The only people who remember me as an athlete were those who saw me play softball and volleyball and the counselors at Camp Michigama where I won the all-around athlete award when I was ten.

Lately I've been thinking about my father. He was a good athlete, too.

We were Fishmans. I still play tennis (though I pay the price the next day). I play Pickle Ball, a lot more forgiving than tennis. And I can pick up a ping-pong paddle and win more than a few points. My dad was a basketball star in high school in Detroit and for a few years at the University of Michigan. He liked showing me where he made the winning basket at Yost Fieldhouse, a venue long retired.

Then there was the day I saw him with a basketball in his hands. We were at my sister's house in the suburbs. She had installed a basket at the end of her driveway and there was my father, shooting hoops with my nephew. But he was shooting poorly, weakly. He used an underhand toss. There was no spring in his wrist or arm. No finesse. He was throwing air balls. I turned away, embarrassed for him.

That's how it would look today if I tried to make the throw from shortstop to first base, let alone across the entire infield from third, which I used to be able to do. I haven't thrown a ball any distance since I tossed tennis balls to my dog in the park. She died 10 years ago and wasn't worth much years before that. I used to have a "good arm." That's what people told me, strangers even. Not anymore.

"It's your hips," my chiropractor says.

"But Dr. John, it's my back that hurts, not my hips."

"Trust me," he said before knocking me into shape. "It's your hips."

"But why does this happen?"

"You're not gonna like what I'm gonna say."

"Go ahead. Lay it on me."

"It's because you're old."

"Older," I tried.

"Old," he said. "Here's my advice. Don't do any yoga. Don't walk. Don't swim. Don't do anything. More business for me. See you in a few weeks."

Cousin Melvin, ten years my senior at 85, likes to say, with a smile, "It all ends badly."

When my friend Ceci, healthy as a horse at 85, was given a thumbs-up prognosis about her overall health ("you could live to a hundred," her doctor announced) she was not thrilled. "Oh, great," she said. "Now I have to start worrying about having enough money to live that long. A new worry."

Gloria Steinem, the poster child for everyone over a certain age, is now 84. She said 50 was a shock, "the end of the center period" of life.

"But once I got over that, sixty was great," she said. "Seventy was great. I loved, I seriously loved aging. I found myself thinking things like, 'I don't want anything I don't have. How great is that?' But eighty? Eighty is about mortality, not aging. Or not just aging."

That's sobering even if people do like to say 80 is the new 60. I'm a lot closer to 80 than the show-off in the observation car. Forget my friends at Tybee, that New Year's Day morning when, thinking I had a daily mantra for the year, I did my last cartwheel.

I'm not the only one thinking about age.

Joan Baez, now 77, is looking at it another way. She is thinking about performing less. She's downsizing. She says she's down to three shirts in her closet. Of course, we don't know how many other closets she has.

Portland was never a city I wanted to move to or visit. Too damp. Too gray. But here it is, on the Empire Builder line. I had time to check it out. I tucked down in my seat in coach, fished out my cell phone, checked out a few hotels and made a reservation. I thought I was dialing the hotel directly but it was through one of those 800-number services. They make me cross. They're so impersonal. That bothered me.

Not long before that, I called another 800-number to donate my old car to Georgia Public Radio except when the operator was taking down the information he said, "So that's Thirty-Eighth Avenue, right?" Knowing it was Thirty-Eighth Street, I said, "You're not from around here, are you?" Bingo. I was talking to someone in Los Angeles. That bothered me, too.

For connectivity in transportation, Portland sets the standard. A city train takes you from the Amtrak station to stops around downtown. That was impressive but I had chosen the wrong hotel. It was all glass, all corporate, all overheated. The windows in the room did not open. Even sleeping in a real bed, off the train, and being able to toss all my stuff around was weird. I missed my cubbyhole in coach, where you live like a tortoise, where everything you need is on your back, where you jam your personal stuff in the meshed compartment on the chair in front of you, where you wake up in a new part of the country every morning, where you nap in the afternoon, if you wish.

Trains are like tortoises, too. You have all you need right with you all the time.

The independent bookstore Powell's, one of my must-visit stops in Portland, was huge; it was overwhelming. It was encouraging to see so many people pawing through books but in the end, there were just, well, too many people. It made me proud of the two independent bookstores we have in Savannah, both small, both eager to find customers what they want. Oh, Book Lady! Oh, E. Shaver! The whole trip to Powell's became worth it when I saw what was hand-lettered on the wide, stretched-out steps between floors: "What do Walt Whitman, Gertrude Stein, Beatrix Potter and D.H. Lawrence have in common? They've all self-published. Are you next?"

I was happy to get back on the train and head for Eugene, a more manageable city. The number of homeless people at the Portland station, hidden under blankets, tucked in sleeping bags, crouched behind cardboard boxes, was sobering. And sad. It did appear that people from the city came by with water and blankets, which is a start, but there has to be a better way to treat people who are down and out.

In Eugene, I would be visiting the parents of a friend of mine I know from Savannah. The parents, Margit and Art, are my age and have visited Savannah many times, but I was always out of town. I called them ahead of time and they invited me to stay with them. I took the bus to Eugene from Portland because the route is so short and I didn't want to use up one of my precious twelve allowable stops on my USA Rail Pass. A few days later, I would board the Coast Starlight for my southbound trip to California. There I would visit a few Detroit Fishman cousins – Bonnie, Nancy and Marcia – who have or are in the process of moving to the West Coast.

Eugene felt more navigable than Portland, more like Savannah. The station had a hometown feel. The wooden, slightly peeling sign above the door reads, "Eugene Depot, to Portland, 123 miles" then on the other side, "to San Francisco, 610 miles," followed by, "elevation, 428 feet." Inside the station the shelf of rack cards held dozens of tourist brochures starting, front and center, with the "Oregon Cannabis Guide and Map." As I waited for my friends I ate at the Morning Glory Café and studied the cannabis map.

I was already liking Eugene. That was before I learned there are no self-service gas stations in Oregon. They have only full-service stations, a boon to the small business owners, which is why, I am told, legislators instituted that. New Jersey is the only other state to do this. I'm not used to state legislators thinking of small businesses.

There are times I yearn for a full-service station.

My first night in Eugene, my friends took me to a house concert. It felt very comfortable. With no offense to my younger friends, it was nice to be in a room with older folks.

On our drive to the concert every other billboard seemed to be a plug for cannabis or a dispensary. One read, "This bud's 4u." Another: "Need weed? Turn left here." A third: "High Eugene, find doctors, storefronts, deliveries, deals." There were more: "Staying in a hotel? Buy an edible or a topical," "Meet your budtender," and "Mynewmeds.com."

After we got back to the house, where I'd spend the next few nights, I settled into my room and checked my email. There was no secret who the advertisers were trying to reach. They know who "we" are. I found the following solicitations: walk-in showers, senior dating options, burial insurance, the joint health center, cannabis pills, face and neck firming cream, senior home care, match 50 + dating, senior apartment locators, crepe erase. I ignored them all and ate the dark chocolate Black Bear Claw my hosts had tucked under my pillow.

In the morning I met Margit's horse, Dice. He's a big fellow. We were waiting for a farrier to come with his bag of tools to clip, shape, trim, file and tend his aging hooves. It was a delicate and tender procedure. I thought of my mother's tough and yellowing toenails in her last few years. I used to crouch down to the floor and cut hers. That was one of my jobs when I visited. But toward the end I had to give it over to a professional. They were just too hard.

Dice is Margit's love.

"He's ancient," she said. "Since they live so long I hesitate to get a new horse, one that would surely outlive me."

When the farrier left, they took me on my first trip to a marijuana dispensary, one of six such storefronts in the city. I had to show some identification so they could check my age. It was strange to be buying a cannabis product on the up and up. For years, I've been in the marijuana world one way or another. I've planted, tended, clipped, picked the plant, smoked. I've never had a "budtender" explain the different strains. I stood quietly and listened as if for the first time and tried to be polite. It was hard. The budtender was so young.

But this *was* a surprise: Each dispensary has an ATM on the property because they deal only in cash. No checks. No credit cards. Not until the FDIC gets with the program and comes on board.

"Welcome," the man at the front desk said when I was checking out. "Let me guess. You've come for the 15 percent Tuesday senior discount, right?"

CHAPTER SIX

HOTEL PENNSYLVANIA

I **NEVER FORGOT MY FANTASY** about staying in the iconic Hotel Pennsylvania, built by the Pennsylvania Railroad in 1919 at the peak of rail popularity. So in between some cross-country excursions I booked a room and hopped up to New York City. Eight hours into the trip, when the Silver Meteor from Savannah was running late, I debated about calling ahead and telling the clerk. It seemed a little overly cautious, a little old-fashioned. I did it anyway. I was excited about staying in this distinguished Beaux-Arts hotel I'd been walking past for years and I didn't want them giving my room away if I were to arrive late. I didn't want to find myself in Manhattan after midnight with no place to stay.

I was heading to New York to surprise my old pal June Millington.

When no one at the hotel answered my third attempt, I did what I thought was the mature thing to do: I left a message saying I'd arrive late.

The hotel sits across the street from Penn Station, a sorry substitute for Grand Central Terminal, which was demolished in the mid-60's. Until I checked I always thought the hotel was a post office or a customs house.

After the 14-hour ride from Savannah, I detrained in the bowels of Penn Station late at night, followed the crowd to the exit sign, rode the steep escalator up to ground level. At that point Madison Square Garden, home to the Knicks and the Rangers, rose several floors higher. In the next week Billy Joel and Phish would give concerts. Outside the station the streets looked just as crowded at night as they did during the day. I squeezed between a line of Yellow Cabs and crossed about a hundred feet to the hotel.

In truth, time of day in New York City does not matter. There's always movement, starting with a bright, blinking neon-yellow digital billboard on my left, at the corner of Seventh Avenue and Thirty-Third Street. Fifty feet up, in front of a half-dozen other billboards, I saw a larger-than-life version of a young Queen Elizabeth and a dapper Prince Phillip advertising *The Crown*, a Netflix series I had just finished watching.

After navigating the street, I pulled open the heavy front doors of the hotel against the wind (they hadn't locked them yet; do they ever lock them? I doubt it), walked ten steps into the lobby. I was in another world. Standing in front of me at one a.m., I saw more people than I had seen in the first two towns in South Carolina we had passed through, Yemassee and Denmark. I was intimidated. I was Eloise, six years old, at the Plaza without a nanny.

Hours earlier, I had listened to a conductor using a familiar Southern vernacular saying, "We're waitin' on a southbound train." We had passed a hand-written sign with directions to a shad fishing contest somewhere near the Pee Dee River. After that we saw posters for the Pig Pickin' Festival in Kingstree, South Carolina. That's when someone across the aisle offered something you'll never hear in a plane: "Teddy Pendergrass was born there. Right there in Kingstree. Yep, my granddaddy done knowed him. Damn shame he got paralyzed in that car accident."

Somewhere between Kingstree and Dillon my phone rang. It was my friend Elaine Longwater from Savannah. She had been thinking about me and wanted to get in touch. When I told her I was on the Silver Meteor headed for New York, she remembered her first trip there in 1960.

I can always count on a story from Elaine. At the time, the train she took was called the East Coast Champion. It operated from 1939 until 1979.

"My father gave me three things to take on the train," she said. Her father's name was Mutsy. "A bucket of fried chicken, a handful of silver dollars and two bags of chestnuts to keep my hands warm, one for each pocket. When I got to New York my heart was beating like a trip hammer. I told the cab driver to open the windows and slow down. I wanted to see everything."

I thought of Elaine inside the hotel as I muscled my way into the line, which is exactly what I found, at 1:30 a.m., on a Tuesday, at the Hotel Pennsylvania. At least 25 travelers stood slouching in front of me, snaking their way toward the front desk to check into their rooms. I took my place behind them and their stacks of luggage but not without complaining. "Couldn't they have more people behind the desk?" I groused to the man in front of me.

He looked up from the screen in his hand long enough to dismiss my complaint with barely a glance. Maybe he didn't speak English.

The line moved. For someone who took the train because she wasn't in a hurry, I was all of a sudden in a hurry. I reached the front desk. The clerk was attentive, efficient. I cooled my jets and settled in. It was 2 a.m. by the time I headed for the elevators. But as with other long train rides, I did not feel wasted or tired. My room was on the fourteenth floor. I asked a heavy-lidded bellman the number of rooms in this seventeen-story hotel. I could tell it wasn't the first time he had been asked this question.

"One thousand seven-hundred seventy," he rattled off.

Whoa. We are not in the Pee Dee anymore.

This hotel has legs. It's got history.

The day it opened, the New York Times wrote, "The incandescent skyline over the heart of New York received a big addition to its candlepower last night when on the gloomiest offshoot of Times Square hundreds of windows were illuminated in the largest tavern in the world, the Hotel Pennsylvania." The story continued: "The first four floors are built in a style to harmonize with the massiveness and dignity of the great railroad building," then known as Grand Central Terminal.

"Included in the hotel's services was a 'servidor.' This is a small wardrobe built into the bedroom doors. The guest may open it from the inside and put his shoes and clothes into it. They will be noiselessly extracted by an attendant from the outside and returned pressed and shined."

Oh, for a servidor. And an attendant.

Some say the hotel's phone number, Pennsylvania-six-five-thousand, the words to a well-known, catchy tune, is the oldest number in continuous use in New York. When the three-letter four-number format was changed in the mid-'40s to two letters and five numbers, the hotel's number went from PEN-5000 to PE6-5000. The Pennsylvania exchange served the area around Penn Station. The Glenn Miller Orchestra made the number famous with its 1940's swing jazz and pop standard song, *Pennsylvania 6-5000*, a tune the Andrews Sisters and big bands played as well.

Miller played in the hotel's famed Café Rouge – now defunct – as did Les Brown's band. In 1944, that's where singer Doris Day introduced the band's *Sentimental Journey*, a song I still remember from seventh grade music class:

Gonna take a sentimental journey
Gonna set my heart at ease
Gonna make a sentimental journey
To renew old memories
Got my bag, got my reservations
Spent each dime I could afford
Like a child in wild anticipation
Long to hear that 'all aboard'
Seven, that's the time we leave, at seven
I'll be waiting up for heaven
Counting every mile of railroad track
That takes me back ...

The size and energy of the place made me want to spend my whole three days in New York within a few blocks. For breakfast, I would go down Sixth Avenue to Murray's for lox and bagels. I would order Chinese. I would sit on the walnut banquette in the commodious hotel lobby and talk to people, starting with Gladys the Gladiator. I met her my first morning there. Wrapped head to toe in three layers, a onesie, a ruck sack and a thermal blanket, Gladys was a terrier mix from Boston. Her owner, who had taken the train, was there to check out the city craft fairs. She never went anywhere without Gladys.

But this was New York. Even if you arrive with an empty dance card, and mine was empty except for surprising June, it's not hard to find ways to fill it up. And I'm not just talking about Korean spicy udon soup, potato knishes or anything from the Halal trucks. I chose an afternoon stage matinee at random: *20th Century Blues*. I sat next to one of the few men in the audience. When I asked him how that felt, he said he hadn't noticed and he didn't really care. "Every Wednesday I sneak out to a matinee. I just pick what seems to be the most interesting. What's the point of living in New York if you don't do this? I had a good day today at the office, too."

He's a venture capitalist, he told me. He explained what that was; it wasn't the first time someone has tried to tell me, but I still didn't get it. I liked talking to him.

Though I never need an excuse to visit New York, I came up with one anyway – to surprise June, a killer guitarist with a huge heart and one of the first women to make it big with her all-woman band, Fanny. Fanny was the first all-female rock band to release an album with a major label, Reprise. In 2017 June wrote an autobiography, *Land of a Thousand Bridges: Island Girl in a Rock and Roll World.*

Now June and partner Ann Hackler run the Institute for the Musical Arts, an all-girls rock-and-roll camp outside Amherst, Massachusetts. When I saw on Facebook she would be playing a fundraiser for the camp at The Cutting Room, a small concert venue on East 32nd Street, some five blocks from the Hotel Pennsylvania, I thought it would be a good time to visit.

I was June's road manager in 1976 when we headed out on a concert tour to college campuses in a cramped VW filled with guitars, speakers, microphones. Because I had another job as a speechwriter for the American Hospital Association in Chicago I had limited time to plan the tour and I wasn't sure what I was doing anyway. We started off with a lot of loose ends. We ended up referring to the tour as "a wing and a prayer." June didn't choose me because I have a good sense of direction; I don't. Or because I was good with details; I'm not. Or because I could figure out the mechanics of sound; I never did. She just knew she could trust me. My life as a road manager was short, but we're still talking and we still love one another. That means something.

At the club, when I realized June and I wouldn't have time to do much talking, I started mentally planning an Amtrak ride to Amherst to see the rock-and-roll camp. Still, it was exciting to see her play and sing. She's just a few years younger than I am, but the passion – and ardor – is still there. That's what I saw when I met her. That's what I saw that night. After forty-one years, it was reaffirming to know my instincts were right.

Two months after my "reunion" with her in New York, June and others were recognized at the Women's International Music Network in Anaheim, California.

I left New York two days later at 11 a.m. on Amtrak's Carolinian. I would make a stop in Durham, North Carolina, to visit a friend before heading back to Savannah. The Carolinian runs daily between Charlotte and New York. After the buzz of New York, it felt good to take a seat in coach and give the reins over to someone else. For the rest of the day I wouldn't have to plan a thing. I wouldn't have to do anything except look out the window, pick up my book, close my eyes or walk to the snack bar.

But I wouldn't have the two seats to myself. That's something you are always hoping for when you board. This time the train was crowded. It was shortly before Christmas.

Right after I sat down, a slender young man slid in next to me. He was on holiday break from college. This was his first long-distance train ride. After an hour or so, under the weak December light and the steady rhythm of the train, we started talking. I guess I was ready for some conversation. I told him about my trip to the Morgan Library in New York, where I saw a letter Jane Austen had written to her 8-year-old niece. Every word was written backward, in code.

He hadn't heard of Jane Austen or the Morgan, but he said both sounded interesting. Then he told me about his mother. She's a white supremacist who lives in Arkansas and goes to the Tony Alamo Christian Church. He hasn't seen her in 11 years. I told him about reuniting with June, someone I hadn't seen in 40 years.

He had been visiting his girlfriend in Baltimore, who, like him, graduated with a degree in physics. "She's about to go off on some naval exploration for a year but only if she can do 50 push-ups. She's in training."

He was on his way to Charlotte to see his father, an accountant. He has one more semester left of college and just finished applying to five doctorate programs. He has a double major, physics and applied mathematics.

"Are you worried about getting a job?" I asked as he brought out his computer and settled in (with headphones) to watch *That 70's Show*, something he said he hadn't had a lot of time to do in the last few years. "I mean, a job in physics? Or math? Anything like that?"

"No," he said. "I'm not worried. I'll just see where life takes me."

I could relate. But if I told him that he might laugh. He'd probably say, "At your age? You don't know where life will take you? Really?"

And I would have to say, "Really. Even at my age."

SMOKING STOPS
IF PERMITEDBY THE
CONDUCTOR,

FORT MADISON, IA   6 : 4
KANSAS CITY, MO.   10 : 1
LA JUNTA,   CO   8 : 1
RATON,   NM   10 : 56 am
ALBUQUERQUE, NM 3 : 55
GALLUP, NM   7 : 08
FLAGSTAFF, AZ   8 : 51 pm
NEEDLES C.A.   12 : 46 p
SAN BERNARDINO,   5 : 32
LOS ANGELES, CA   8 : 15

CHAPTER SEVEN

IOWA AND MIKE

IOWA WAS NOT IN MY SIGHTS. Where is Iowa anyway?

"A roundtrip ticket to Des Moines, please."

Where is Des Moines?

"And the date of your return?"

"Today."

"Today? So you'll only be staying half an hour?"

"That's right."

That's what you do when you're 22, new in town, lonely, depressed, unhappy with your job and not a shopper. You get on a train. To anywhere.

It was a cash transaction. Or maybe a check. People took checks from strangers back then. It was a more trusting time. I didn't have a credit card.

It was 1966. I was a first-year English teacher in Chicago. I had no idea what I was doing with my life. A stack of papers sat on a makeshift coffee table in my Hyde Park apartment waiting to be graded, something I didn't want to do. I was four years older than most of my students and doing this job only because that's what women did back then. We taught. We worked in the post office. We became social workers. We traveled in Europe. As teachers, we wore skirts. Pants were forbidden. It would not be my life's work. I knew that.

That gloomy November Sunday, I also knew I needed to be somewhere else for the day, and this train, which was leaving in ten minutes, would get me there – somewhere – and then back in time to teach the next day.

Intuitively I knew the train ride would ground me. It still does. It would keep me safe from the rest of the world. It still does that, too. For however short a time, it would provide company. I'm friendly but not social. There was something about that lonely whistle that expressed how I felt. At least I could feel lonely around other people.

In the summer, when I was growing up in Michigan, we would take the train to camp in Wisconsin. I remember eating Junior Mints, Mary Janes and red pistachios, then leaving red fingermarks on the Archie & Veronica comic books I was reading. Pistachios were once red. Somewhere along the line, they stopped dyeing them. I loved overnight camp, the chance to be away from home eight weeks. I couldn't wait. I don't especially remember the train. I just wanted to get to camp.

I'm not in such a hurry anymore.

This teaching thing was my first job, my first time living in a big city. I was uncertain about everything: the kids, the principal, myself, the lessons I was supposed to teach. I was adrift, unmoored. I'd stop and eat donuts before getting to school, arriving with powdered sugar on my dress. After school I would cross Lake Shore Drive from my apartment and walk along the oversized rocks covered in ice in the winter. Other times I'd get on the elevated train and ride to the North Side, then back to the South Side. I had no direction. I hadn't discovered reading as a means of distraction. Or weeding. I was not a bar person.

I had no diversions – no cellphone (there were none), no Google to check on people of the past (there was hardly time for a past), no friends (my room-mate, a friend from college, wanted to move out and live on her own) and no idea what to do next.

I was young.

The train was my religion.

I had met some fellow teachers I liked, but their lives, like mine, like the 60's, the decade we inhabited, were in transition. One moved with her sister to Paris. Another took off with a high school student from our school in her VW bug, drove to San Francisco and started driving a cab in a female-owned company. A third, a woman, became a love interest of mine, which caused great distress and confusion.

Des Moines was hilly with beautiful high bluffs. That's all I remember, except I knew I was in good hands on the train for a few hours. I didn't have to do a thing, a feeling I still embrace.

The mournful – or was it sad? – sound of the train whistle, still a thrill to hear even if it's coming from a freight train carrying highly flammable explosives, speaks of distant places beyond all I know. Its sounds give answers to questions I do not know to ask. Time seems to disappear. I can drift.

My random trip to Iowa predated Amtrak by about five years. Today, I can't even find a train to Des Moines from Chicago. The schedule has changed but Amtrak probably uses the same tracks.

Those were the last-gasp days of trains.

In my parents' day, everyone took the train. My mother and father took one to Los Angeles for their honeymoon. That would have been in the mid-'30s.

I doubt the train they took and the ones I take look anything alike.

My parents divorced in 1966. By the time I asked about their life together or the promise of that first train ride, my mom had no interest in discussing the subject.

"Why would I want to talk about him?" my mother asked, seriously dumbfounded by the question about her married life, or of the promise of that first train ride together.

"He's my father," I said. "I'm interested."

That went nowhere. She offered very little about their life together – or the train. Maybe she didn't remember. I've seen their wedding picture, the night before the honeymoon, the night before boarding the train. But that's all.

It never occurred to me to ask my father.

I always thought there would be time later. Big mistake.

I thought of their cross-country adventure and the style in which they traveled (no coach for them) when I happened by chance to see one of those fancied-up, old-fashioned, pre-Amtrak private railroad cars that people, like my parents, might have boarded. I was getting off the Capitol Limited at Penn Station in downtown Pittsburgh, headed to a friend's house in Squirrel Hill to keep her company after hip surgery. I always like excuses to take the train and to step into someone else's life, however briefly. When I offered, she said she could use the help. My train pulled in from Washington D.C. at 8:30 at night. About an hour before we arrived, a voluble car attendant, walking the aisles, burbling over with excitement, told anyone who would listen about the private car our train was pulling. It belonged to Bennett Levin. That meant nothing. None of us had heard of Mr. Levin.

"He's a railroad nut," he said, clearly excited to be on the same train with him. "He's traveling with some bigwig from Amtrak."

For $2.10 per mile ($1,000 minimum), Amtrak will haul your private car. It's a moneymaker for Amtrak. It's a win-win. These cars, no matter how fancy, are useless by themselves. They need the power of a locomotive. Levin is the quintessential rail enthusiast with the money to back up his interests.

"But why would someone want their own railroad car?" I asked the car attendant, still confused.

He barely took a breath before answering, "Why would someone want their own plane or an expensive car? Because the man loves trains."

Now I was curious. When we detrained I walked back in the bowels of the dark station to have a look at the car in the rear. The heavy patterned floor-to-ceiling curtains were pulled open. The interior was bathed in a warm and friendly light. People leaned back on easy chairs drinking cocktails, looking jolly.

The dining room table was set. The tablecloth appeared to be fine cotton, not the heavy white paper Amtrak passengers get. The cutlery looked heavy, definitely not plastic. I spotted mahogany paneling on the walls. Brocade sofas, more like banquettes, lined the perimeter. The ornate chandeliers were lit. Later I read some cars have marble sinks and fireplaces.

I was looking into another time, another era.

On this particular night, Levin was traveling with two of his historic beauties, the "Warrior Ridge" and "The Liberty Limited," their names painted on the sides of the cars.

Earlier the conductor told us Levin's other car, the "Pennsylvania 120," transported Bobby Kennedy's body in 1968 from New York's Grand Central Station to Washington D.C.'s Union Station for burial at Arlington Cemetery.

I took the escalator up to the ground level. After seeing Levin's exquisitely appointed train, I expected to head upstairs and find an equally grand old train station. I didn't. Pittsburgh's Amtrak station is a whisper of what it was. The business takes place underground. Even the Uber driver couldn't find the address. The stunning twelve-story building Daniel Burnham designed and built in the early 1900s was intended to show off an important and busy city. Today it's been converted to condominiums. It's called The Pennsylvanian. With the decline in passenger travel it was either tear it down or team up with Amtrak.

The dramatic rotunda with corner pavilions of brick and grayish brown terra cotta and the grand entrance still exist but not for passengers. Now they are for tenants. At one time the rotunda provided sheltered turning spaces for carriages to pull in and out. The building's vaulted skylights and stained-glass windows still remain.

With only four daily trains in and out of Pittsburgh, Burnham's building – like Levin's cars – is a relic, a monument to the past. It's an antique, like a rotary phone, a flashbulb, a pencil sharpener, a typewriter ribbon.

Sometimes I think I belong on that list. Trains certainly do.

On that same trip, I got into a conversation with a father-son combination in the snack bar area, a section that has no ambiance, no romance. It's a place where train attendants do their paperwork and listen to their walkie-talkies. The only color I saw on the walls was another poster for Joe Biden's new book, *Promise Me, Dad: A Year of Hope, Hardship, and Purpose.*

Today's sterile snack bar is a far cry from the old smoking lounge, which was filled with fumes and fun. The father and son were on their way to a funeral in Pittsburgh. A newspaper was spread out in front of them. This was the son's first funeral.

"OK, it's your first funeral," I said, "but have you ever known anyone who died?"

"Nope," he said.

The father and I exchanged a glance. Then I asked the elder, who might have been 45, if he deletes people who have died from the contact list in his phone or, if he still had one, from his address book.

"No," he said. "I leave them there, in my phone and my address book."

"Me, too," I said. "I like seeing their names."

"It's messed up, but it's what we got," said the father.

A few months later, I was thinking about my own father when I realized I'd be in Chicago on a layover between trains. I texted my nephew to see if he had time to meet me. Mike's a high-end real estate guy who loves to work. When he had left the company he worked with for many years, he tried staying home in his northwest Detroit suburban house. That wasn't for him. He can't sit still that long. He put out some feelers and hooked up with another multinational company based in Chicago.

He was quite helpful to me after my mom passed away in 2010 and one of the few people I know still alive who knew my father. He died 25 years ago. The further away I get from my parents, the more important family like Mike become.

Now he spends the week in Chicago, sometimes riding the Hiawatha to Milwaukee and back for a one-day meeting.

"That's one of the better routes," I told him. "Something like seven trips a day with a 97 percent on-time rate."

"How do you know that?" he said, surprised.

"I just do," I said. I like to impress my nephew.

"There's something like fifty trains in and out of Chicago a day," I continue, pleased with myself. I certainly don't know all the routes by any stretch, but since everything I want to take seems to start in Chicago – not the most convenient for me in Savannah – I did check that out one day.

On the weekend, Mike takes Amtrak's Wolverine line back to his home in Detroit. I increased my cred by telling him the Wolverine runs on-time 75 percent of the time.

I never figured him for a train guy. He rides in business, a class I never knew existed. He says it works for him, "though not worth the additional cost." They are designated as quiet cars. He can get some work done.

To my surprise, Mike made time for me.

My train from Dallas on the Texas Eagle got in at 4:30 in the afternoon; my next leg on the Capitol Limited was scheduled to leave at 6:40 p.m. We met at a coffee shop that faced the Chicago River next to a high-rise in a high-dollar part of town, not far from the Amtrak station.

We talked about his kids, his houses, my life, my gardens and some random family members. Then, as it usually does, my father's name came up.

"Manny saved me after my dad died," he said. "I was eleven. He'd pop over and take me and my friends to all the games, football, baseball, hockey. Then we'd go out for ice cream. He really got me into sports."

"That was when he was writing columns for the Birmingham Eccentric, right?" I asked, remembering the local newspaper. "It's so strange how we ended up doing the same thing. He really couldn't do much else. I can't either to tell you the truth. I used to have some of those columns. He gave them to me. But I'll be darned if I can find them. It's just too weird that we both ended up writing columns."

"I have some tucked away in my attic," Mike said. "I'll send them to you."

An hour later we fought the five o'clock Chicago foot traffic and headed for Union Station. He pulled my suitcase as we walked down LaSalle Street. We hugged and parted, his tailored blue suit fading into the crowd. When I got back on the train, still musing about our visit, I got to thinking about something he said, so I texted him. "Did you really call my father, your grandfather, 'Manny?'"

"I did," Mike answered.

How did I not remember this?

CHAPTER EIGHT

LATE TRAINS AND OLD FRIENDS

TO ITS CREDIT, AMTRAK PUBLISHES what it calls a "train route on-time performance" ranking. The results run the gamut. Not surprisingly the shortest routes get the best numbers. As mentioned, the latest score for the 86-mile Hiawatha between Chicago and Milwaukee is 95 percent, while California's Capitol Corridor, a 168-mile route between San Jose and Sacramento, is on time 91 percent of the time. Out of 34 Amtrak routes, those two are the only ones in the nineties. The three bringing up the rear are the Lake Shore Limited, running between Chicago and New York City at 48 percent; the Crescent, on time 42 percent of the time as it heads from New Orleans to New York City, and finally the Silver Service, which runs between Miami and New York. It notches a dismal 39 percent on-time record.

These are discouraging numbers for people in a hurry. But there's a reason: freight trains. These privately held companies – Union Pacific, BNSF, CSX and Norfolk Southern, all names of the past in the world of railroads – own most of the tracks, rolling stock and locomotives (or engines). The numbers between privately held freight trains and publicly owned passenger trains aren't even close. As track-owners, freight companies call most of the shots. At some point, passenger folks gave over or sold existing tracks and right-of-way to freight. They stopped adding new track, stopped building more engines, stopped buying more land. With most of the West already developed (thanks in part to the railroad), commerce put its money behind trucks, cars and highways. For people with money and sophistication, air travel took over. Trains, be damned. Anyway, they're always late, right?

But sometimes, hand to God, a train does leave on time. Maybe even a minute early. When that happens – since the depot is a 20-minute drive away from your house and the parking lot a 50-step walk from the tracks – you can become a little too casual. Then, if you are a minute (or five) late, you might find you are the only one standing on the platform watching the Palmetto No. 90 crawl away. That is when you think, "I can't believe what just happened."

Your first thought? Run! Run! Maybe if I run fast enough someone will see me. Someone will yell, "Stop the train. There's one more person." You think, maybe I can make a flying leap, hobo-style, and swing onto the baggage car. Except there are no open platforms on passenger cars. There's nothing to hold on to. That kind of acrobatic act happens only in the movies – or when you're under twenty. To watch a train pull away is not quite as abrupt an experience as running through an airline terminal only to come face to face with a snotty, hard-hearted gate agent standing there, obdurate, implacable while the two of you can see the plane on the runway. But it is final. It is irreversible. The plane won't wait, and that train is not going to stick around either. It is not going to put on the brakes until you catch up.

The whole late thing was my fault. When Deloris, a Savannah attendant I knew from previous trips, a nice woman, offered to drive me in one of those golf carts to the train, which was waiting and poised on the tracks, I got huffy and sarcastic and said, "What, you don't think I can walk all that way?" I got defensive. I was thinking of earlier train trips when attendants stop to offer rides to people, such as myself, who might be a bit older. Pride goeth before a fall.

Still, missing a train is abrupt. It's not like missing a subway connection when another is on the way. It's embarrassing, especially when you walk back into the train depot pulling your suitcase with everyone, including Deloris, staring at you.

Especially since trains never seem to be on time.

Except when you're catching a train at its point of origin. Then the on-time performance rating is irrelevant. The Palmetto, which I had just missed, originates in Savannah. It is never late.

"The good news?" said the man behind the glass counter. "The next train is cheaper."

And the bad news?

"It leaves at one-thirty a.m."

To someone who goes to bed around ten or eleven, the world looks a whole lot different at one-thirty a.m. What do people do between eleven and one a.m.? There is less traffic, I'll give the night owls that. On Amtrak's behalf, the station is more crowded, the average age a couple of decades younger. At night, the mint green walls of the station look brighter and greener. The inside of the one-thirty a.m. train, the Silver Star – this train was also on time – looked different, too. People are sprawling, slouching and straddling. No one looks their best. No one is reading. That's when you slap on your sleep mask, check out for a few hours and hope you don't miss your eight a.m. stop in Cary, N.C. From Cary, it's a four-hour wait for the No. 75 Piedmont to Durham.

There's no muss, no fuss on trains at night. The car attendant dispenses with the usual announcement: "please be careful when moving from car to car," "please wear your shoes," "please remember to turn off your devices by ten p.m."

I was on my way to visit a friend in Durham. It wasn't a pleasure trip. His partner of nearly fourteen years had passed away four days earlier. Pete was 59 years old. No long illness. Nothing expected. Just a lingering pulmonary infection. It was sudden. It was shocking. It was final. It reminded me of what I heard at another recent funeral: "In the midst of life, we are in death."

"We lost him," Gene said a few days earlier when I had called to check on his progress.

I'll go up to see him, I thought. I wasn't sure what I could do to help or how he would respond to the offer, but I made it anyway. He seemed pleased. "Yes, yes. Come up," he said.

How could I not go? I had the time.

Then I missed the train. After I changed my ticket to a departure in the wee hours and before I headed back to my car, I sat down on one of the plastic benches in Savannah's station. I needed to regroup. I bit the bullet and called Gene with the news. It reminded me of the time I was being hauled off to jail for keying a policeman's car in a pique of anger over receiving yet another ticket, this time for parking on the wrong side of the street during street sweeping night.

"Gene," I said from the holding station after I had been booked. "Do you have $75?"

"Yes," he said.

"In cash?"

"Yes, but why?"

"It's bail money," I said. "I need to get out of jail and I'm not talking Monopoly."

He came right over.

This was different. I made myself stop thinking of that.

I focused on the call. I just came right out and said it.

"I missed the train," I blurted out, close to tears. I felt terrible. I let him down. Maybe I missed the train on purpose. Maybe it's true what people say: There are no accidents. Maybe it was presumptuous to think I could help him in the first place. I knew I was nervous about going, uncertain about what I could do, afraid I would do nothing but cry. And who needs that?

"You did what?" he said in that exaggerated high voice friends can use with one another as if to say, "You idiot!"

Then he laughed, maybe his first laugh since Pete's death.

"You missed the train?"

Then I laughed. I hated missing the train but I was grateful to offer comic relief. The whole time I visited him in Durham he told the story again and again to friends and neighbors, how I missed the train – "no one misses a train!" – how I contemplated running to make it stop, how I had to catch another one leaving at one-thirty, "in the morning."

At one point, I thought about chucking the train plans and driving. Maybe it would be faster. But what's the hurry, I thought. I would take the train, even if it was during a time of night I never considered traveling. But that's the thing about trains that people forget: Except for overseas flights, trains push on through the night. They don't stop long to refuel, to make connections, to sleep. Three a.m., four a.m., it means nothing to them. They travel at their own slow and steady pace, laying on the horn at crossings, navigating those curves, stopping to pick up one or two people waiting in the dark at some unattended station, stopping again to drop off a handful of passengers, the tortoise versus the hare.

While it might be cheaper to ride in the middle of the night, I felt cheated. I like passing through Americana, easing into a one-story station in the middle of some small town not too far from a hardware store, a post office, a county museum, a courthouse or, in the case of Dillon, South Carolina, a town clock that towers over a new brick platform. I like watching family and friends waving goodbye until the last possible moment. I don't have to know them to get teary.

On my return trip to Savannah I made sure I paid attention to the time. I didn't want to miss this leg. I took a pen and wrote 9:42 on the top of my hand. I would not be late. From Durham – a lovely station in a converted tobacco warehouse (no TV) – I took the No. 80 Carolinian to Wilson, N.C.

With a lifelike mosaic sculpture by artist Michael Brown of a woman sitting on a bench waiting for a train, it's hard not to like the Wilson station. It's a good thing. I had four hours before catching the Palmetto back to Savannah.

That may seem like a long layover, but to me the depot in Wilson felt like a safe zone, quiet and secure. It has seven wooden pews, three long ones in the middle, four along the side. It was peaceful. If you are waiting for a plane in an airport, the noise is constant. A cleaning cart with a wonky wheel. Herb Alpert trumpets as background music. Announcements: "The plane is late due to a crew swap in Atlanta." "This is the pilot with an update. One of the brakes is not operating." "Now we're waiting for the catering truck." "All right folks, I'm afraid we're moving gates."

In the train depot, I could sit and reflect on the trip. This is my happy place, I thought, riding a train, waiting for a train, sharing space with strangers on a train.

For my three-day stay in Durham, I kept Gene company as he pawed through piles of papers, fielded phone calls from friends, greeted neighbors coming over with food. The temperature dipped so I wore a sweatshirt of Pete's that said "Duke."

"Take it with you," Gene said. We went to a bookstore. We walked the dog. I held open garbage bags as he jammed in stuff to recycle, give away or throw away. I watched him slip important documents into the plastic sleeves of a notebook. We sat across from one another in the living room and each one of us chose a Flannery O'Connor short story to read out loud, *Good Country People* and *Revelation*. We turned in to bed by 10:00.

In the Wilson railroad station, a perfect square, a perfect size, I perched on the wooden pew, my feet barely touching the floor, and thought maybe I should have stayed longer. I hated leaving but I knew other friends were coming to be with him.

The station, a one-story red brick building reconstructed in 1996, followed the original architecture of the 1924 station with Spanish terra cotta roof tiles. The station was the center of growth for Wilson in the nineteenth century, as were many depots in other small towns. Wilson was known as the city of beautiful trees. It was incorporated in 1849 as a farm market. Later it became known as a producer of bright leaf tobacco.

For the first hour, four of us sat in the station. You could hear every cough, every crinkle of candy wrapping, every shoe squeak as someone new walked in. Like Durham, there was no TV. A man sat behind the Amtrak counter reading a newspaper. The phone did not ring. An older gentleman, his hands folded on his lap, asked me where I had been.

"I went to help someone bury his husband," I said.

"Me, too," he answered without skipping a beat, paying no attention to the same-sex reference. "Except it was my sister. Damn, that hurt."

An hour into the wait for the No. 89 Palmetto (by this time I had learned the even numbers go north, the odd numbers head south) I noticed SaYum Jamaican food a few puddles across Nash Street East. It featured recipes from "Pearl Bell's repertoire." I ordered curry chicken, rice and beans, cabbage and fried plantains: $6.40. I told them to wrap it well so I wouldn't break into it right away. SaYum stands for "save a youth," a local organization. I didn't ask what that meant.

When we finally boarded for my ride home the late afternoon light lingered. We had "sprung forward" into Daylight saving time. I read. I closed my eyes. I stared out the window. I had both seats to myself.

"Kind of empty," I mentioned to the car attendant.

"Mondays," he said. "Never many people on Monday."

By the time we hit Charleston I woke with a start, afraid I had missed my stop. It was so dark and there were so few lights for reference I couldn't tell if we were moving or standing still. We approached Savannah close to 9:30, about twenty minutes late.

"Watch yourself," the attendant said. "The steps in Savannah are a little higher. If you have baggage, wait next to the soda machine."

On my way to the parking lot I saw the same attendant who had changed my ticket a few days earlier.

"Everything OK?" he asked.

I gave him the thumbs up. Everything is A-OK. I left in the dark. I returned in the dark.

CHAPTER NINE

PANTSUIT NATION AND OTHER INTERLUDES IN WASHINGTON, D.C.

ON THE MORNING OF THE WOMEN'S MARCH, a couple months after the dismal 2016 election, we pulled into Washington D.C.'s Union Station ahead of schedule. The train was packed. We had ridden the Silver Meteor from Savannah. Usually there's nothing too meteor-like for this Miami-to-New York train. It makes 25 stops between South Florida and Manhattan. Its sluggish 48 percent on-time rating doesn't help matters.

This early arrival was an anomaly. But this was not an ordinary day. Instead of the usual ten stops between Savannah and Washington, D.C., through Georgia, South Carolina, North Carolina and Virginia, there were only five. So many people, mostly women but not all, had made reservations ahead of time to go to the march, which meant the train didn't have to interrupt its pokey pace to stop and let people board. There were no available tickets to buy. The train could just keep on rolling.

Some of us made our reservations as soon as we heard about the march, before we had time to finish sitting Shiva about the election results, before we had time to move past any of Elisabeth Kübler-Ross' stages of grief. Make no mistake: We were in mourning. The dowdy pantsuits we had bought for a dollar as a joke at the Salvation Army thrift shop, to wear to election parties, still lay sprawled on our bedroom floors. After hearing the results, we didn't have the energy to pick them up, pack them up, hang them up, or pass them along to anyone who might want to really wear them. We didn't want to deal with it. The night of the election we went to sleep in a funk, before 10, before all the results were in. What was the point of staying up?

By the time of the march we were still in a funk.

Almost a year later, I had had a happier moment on a train to New York, also political related. It was December 2017, the night of the special election in Alabama, when Doug Jones, a Democrat no one had heard of, was running against Roy Moore, the reprobate Republican with a penchant for teenage girls and lying. Two one-syllable, gentile-sounding names, two white men, both from Alabama. I'll admit it: For the longest time, I couldn't keep them straight. I wasn't following the election. I didn't know the good guy from the bad guy.

Since we can now get Internet connection on the train (most of the time) I started checking on the election results early in my ride, this despite my contention I take the train to check out of news, life, responsibility.

By the time this New York-bound train reached Washington, D.C., most of the Southern passengers had gotten off. The train was quieting down. Joseph, the man behind me who had been giving advice to his best buddy for nearly an hour ("She ain't called you back yet? Put the stove on 500 and let her simmer"), detrained in Rocky Mount, North Carolina. Hallelujah.

Josephine, who was so afraid she'd miss the funeral because she was "carrying Granny's pound cake," got off in Richmond. I'm sorry for your loss, I wanted to say because by that time I had heard all about it. I hope the cake makes it. And the very pregnant woman who spent most of the time in and out of the bathroom? She made it to Fredericksburg, Virginia, without giving birth.

In D.C., we picked up a different crowd. They were suits from government, still in ties and high heels. They were young. They'd already had a few drinks. They were liberal. And they were following the election in Alabama with great interest. By this time those four newcomers and I practically had the car to ourselves.

"Ahead by three," I heard someone yell. "Woo hoo."

I couldn't stay silent.

"No," I said, looking at my computer. "It says here he's behind by four."

I got out of my seat and joined them. This was important.

"Where'd you see that?" I asked. I was questioning people who were plugged in to the latest of everything. Who was I kidding? Analog meets technocrat.

By then the election had been called. Our guy won.

The two couples reached in a bag and pulled out some Champagne, a big no-no on Amtrak. We kept that quiet. They handed me a glass. One year after the presidential election this felt like the first bright moment. Could it really be true?

That was an isolated moment. Eleven months earlier, right after the disappointing election of 2016, we were not so jubilant. But we were traveling to meet our tribe. That mild day in January, the day of the Women's March, we would be part of a huge mass of like-minded people, if just for the day. We needed a gathering like this in the 60's when we marched against the Vietnam War and for civil rights. We needed it in the 90's to protest the Iraq War, policies against gays and lesbians, attitudes toward women. We needed it now.

The night before we left for the post-election march, I remembered someone I had met on an earlier train. It was on the Capitol Limited. We were sharing a breakfast table somewhere between Chicago and D.C. I was returning from Santa Fe. Amtrak being the convoluted system it is I had to go to Chicago first before catching two more trains back to Savannah. You have to be crazy to take a train with those kind of cockamamie connections, crazy or someone with some time to spare. I guess I fit both categories.

There were four of us at the table that morning. One man, an art dealer, was a Palestinian from Montreal. He ate quickly and left. The second was a lawyer who represents coal miners. He was reading, *And We Are Not Saved: A History of the Movement as People*, written by Debbie Louis. He takes the train between Morgantown, West Virginia, and Washington, D.C. "A good time to work on briefs," he said.

But I was focused on the third man. He looked sharp in a narrow string tie and suit jacket. He was from Laramie, Wyoming. He was heading to Washington as a member of the Louisa Swain Foundation. He didn't seem anxious to talk, but I was curious. I waited for our plates to be cleared, our coffee refilled, then I said, "Louisa who?"

"Miss Swain," he started, leaving off the first name in respect for the dead, sounding as if everyone should know her, "was the first woman to vote in a general election, in 1870."

That got our attention.

That's not all, he said. "There were three other firsts that year: the first woman to serve on a jury, the first woman to act as a bailiff and the first woman chosen for a judicial position."

All in Wyoming.

When I got back to my seat I was suspicious. Maybe he was just creating a scenario. I looked up the foundation. There it was. Its purpose is to promote the concepts of democracy, human rights, suffrage, justice, community, courage and strength of character. The goals for that group in Wyoming in 1870 couldn't be closer to what we wanted to do in Washington when we went to march in 2017. The struggle has always been with us.

That morning at breakfast, before I could be sure he and the foundation were on the level, all I could think to say was, "So much for ignoring what happens in flyover states."

He didn't laugh. I doubt he heard me or was listening. Oh, we are so bicoastal, I thought, so snobbish. The left coast, the right coast, nothing in between. I thought about him at the Women's March, but while I didn't spot anyone from the Louisa Swain Foundation, I did see representation from Wyoming.

As the train shimmied out of Savannah the night before the Women's March, I watched my friend Sari across the aisle.

She was squirming, trying to get comfortable. This was her first march. How could this be? At fifty, she's an outspoken activist with a proper sense of outrage. She's very smart, from Los Angeles, a graduate of UC Berkeley. This was her first train ride, too. She curled up, leaned against the window, pushed the seat back, kicked out the foot rest and experimented with stretching. It was difficult.

"You SLEEP in coach?" she queried as if to say, "Are you crazy?"

A little while later I saw her head for the bathroom carrying the large backpack she had brought.

"You really can leave your stuff on your seat, you know," I said, hoping I wasn't sounding too much like her mother, although as I think about it that's exactly what a cautious mother would say.

"Really?"

Really. I have never heard of any thievery on the train. People sleep with their suitcases up top on the shelves or, in the case of long distance trains, on the lower level. They go to the dining room without their bags. They sit for hours in the lounge free of their possessions, none of which, by the way, are ever checked upon boarding.

I didn't think she'd ever take another train ride, but a year later, in 2018, after the horrendous school shootings in Parkland, Florida, she surprised me. She took her daughter, then 12, on the train to D.C. for the March for Our Lives. That time they spent the night in a hotel before heading back the next day.

I have not always been happy with Amtrak and its crazy scheduling. Who has time to wait from seven in the morning until three in the afternoon to make a travel connection? This is what happens when you pull into D.C., from Savannah. None of the connecting trains leave until three in the afternoon.

But I've made my peace with it. This was Washington, D.C., after all, where the National Mall is minutes away from the station, where anything can happen. Now I look forward to the time. During one layover, hunting around for something to do, I hitched up with a large group of protesters before I even knew what they were protesting or where they were going. It turns out they were doctors, nurses and health care workers, carrying signs with great enthusiasm. I followed them to the steps of the Supreme Court, which was about to hear arguments in King v. Burwell over the Affordable Care Act.

Another time, when I arrived on a beautiful spring Sunday morning, the train was on time. None of the free museums was open yet. I must have looked flummoxed because a lovely woman stopped and asked if she could help.

When I verbalized my dilemma, asking if she had any recommendations for breakfast, she didn't hesitate. "Jimmy T's. On East Capitol and 5th. It's kind of a greasy spoon on the first floor of a row house. The owners live upstairs, and they serve breakfast all day. Then you can go to some museums. C'mon. I'm heading that way."

That's all I needed to hear. Margot, a life coach and a Pilates teacher with a Ph.D. in preventive mental health, was now my tour guide. On our way to East Capitol, as we passed tulips, cherry blossoms, dogwood and irises – my second spring, since Savannah had already moved into summer – my mood improved.

Jimmy T's was perfect. A little overpriced, but the chatter was lively, the mugs mismatched and the waffles an inch thick.

From there she pointed me to the Eastern Market on 8th Street. It's housed in an elongated redbrick 19th-century building and the parking lot of an adjacent public school. I bought a $3 vegetarian egg roll from a street vendor, wandered a little more and sat for a little nap under Louise Bourgeois' spider sculpture outside the National Gallery of Art.

After that I thought I might as well walk to the White House. On my way, I passed the Folger Shakespeare Library, where I entered a lottery for a ticket to the afternoon performance, followed by a procession for Palm Sunday, the front of the Botanical Gardens and a couple hundred runners who stopped every now and then to have their pictures taken in front of a statue.

That's when someone stopped and asked, "Does your name start with an 'N' or 'B'?" They were on some kind of urban scavenger hunt or a giant game of Trivial Pursuit. It looked like fun, but by then I had a train to catch.

It must have been my lucky day. That night on the train I got a call: I had won two free tickets to *Cyrano de Bergerac* at the Shakespeare theater. I wish Margot had been around. I could have given them to her.

As often as I've taken the Silver Meteor to Washington, D.C., and complained about it – the paucity of items in the "snack bar," the overheated cars or the chatter of some of the passengers – I've come to embrace it.

The night before the Women's March, too keyed up to sleep, I looked out the window as we passed long patches of dark woods, the occasional red blinking light at a road crossing, empty storefronts, a handful of simple Baptist churches. I slept through Petersburg, Richmond and Fredericksburg, all in Virginia. By the time we got to Alexandria I could smell the coffee. Someone walking down the aisle had beaten me to the snack bar. My young friend across the aisle looked dazed.

On the ride home, I was high. We had marched with 400,000 people. There were 408 marches across the United States and in 81 other countries, two million people total.

There was humor. There were costumes. There was art. Pink vagina suits, Rosie the Riveter outfits, a "NO" poncho, "Nasty Women" t-shirts, umbrellas painted to resemble nipples, vulva-shaped hats, groups of women dressed in white intended to be suffragettes.

"Remember, the Constitution doesn't begin with 'I the President.' It begins with 'We the People,'" said Gloria Steinem from the main stage.

We may not like the look, but we are the Pantsuit Nation. At least 50 people came to march from Savannah. We were easy to spot. We carried signs painted by hometown folk artist Panhandle Slim (aka Scott Stanton), who gave them away. Mine was a line drawing and a quote from Nina Simone. It read: "I'll tell you what freedom is to me: No fear." There was a drawing of Ruth Bader Ginsburg ("I dissent."), Eleanor Roosevelt ("Understanding is a two-way street"), Frida Kahlo ("At the end of the day we can endure much more than we think we can").

It took stamina, bags of almonds and raisins, and a good bladder to stand shoulder to shoulder in the mosh pit. We landed somewhere between the Museum of Native American History and the gray bureaucratic Sam Rayburn House Office Building as speakers delivered their take on the world as we know it. From Michael Moore, we heard instructions to talk to our representative in Congress every day. From Muhammed Ali's daughter we heard, "Don't get frustrated, get involved." We heard admonitions. "Sometimes pressing 'send' is not enough," warned Steinem. We heard reminders. "We are agents of history. History cannot be deleted like web pages," said the once-fiery, always-wise Angela Davis.

Eventually we wiggled out of the scrum, broke free and paraded down Pennsylvania Avenue to cheers from people standing on the balcony of the Newseum. We heard speeches from the mothers of young black men who had been killed on the streets. We chanted, "This is what Democracy looks like," over and over again.

By late afternoon, exhausted, spent, exhilarated, we trudged back to the station with our pink "pussy hats" in time to get on the 7:15 p.m. returning Silver Star that was due back in Savannah at 7 a.m. We carried our pink hats, knitted beanies with cat ears.

Riding up and riding back, the train was our clubhouse, our respite, our womb, our world. We were empowered. Even the train attendant on the

Miami-bound Number 97 could feel it. When we woke up, groggy, tired and ready to detrain, she cautioned everyone to look around and "get your belongings." Then she asked, "But do you think he heard? Do you think the President heard?"

I'm not sure he heard anything above the sound of his own voice. But we spoke loudly and in unison. That's a start.

CHAPTER TEN

A LETTER TO THE PRESIDENT OF AMTRAK

IF SPEAKING UP AND MARCHING for a cause has purpose, so does letter-writing. Why not go right to the top? This is my letter to the new chief at Amtrak:

Dear Mr. Richard Anderson,

Welcome aboard! I hear you are moving over from Delta Air Lines, where everyone said you did such a good job. Before that it was United Healthcare. Wow. Impressive. Two mammoth, complex, challenging industries. I heard most of this news from Victoria, the car attendant on the Capitol Limited out of Chicago.

She's excited about you coming on board. Me too. There are so many great things about the train. Like Victoria. Flight attendants don't hold a candle to train attendants. Airline people never have anything nice to say. They're plastic. And they're not particularly helpful. Oh sure, they tell us we can unbuckle our seat belts or they might say, "Keep your seatbelts firmly secured." Is there any other way? Then they say we can walk around if we wish. But, I want to ask, where should we walk? They act as if we're doing them a favor when we squeeze into our seats.

I know you're pretty busy with numbers and tracks and switches and health care regulations, all the things it takes to run a big company, especially since we all know how passenger trains have to take a distant second to freight trains even though passenger trains are supposed to be given priority. Except it never seems to work out that way, does it? Don't get me wrong. I would much rather have trains than trucks moving freight. Trucks are tough to see over on the highway. They drive so fast. They are bullies; they make it so hard for people driving cars.

But I do think there is room on the railroad tracks for trains to carry freight and passengers, even though anyone can see there seems to be more profit in "product" than people. And we are a country that loves product. Check out all the self-storage units you pass on the train. The thing about trains is: We travelers don't seem to mind disruptions. We don't always like it, but we understand. Sometimes conductors even let you out on the platform for a smoke or to get some fresh air while the issue-of-the-moment is being addressed. It's not like sitting on a plane, tightly packed like sardines when you're circling the airport waiting for an available runway, an interminable process that can go on for hours in that contained capsule of space when you feel anyone can go postal, any time.

Not so on a train. Maybe you've forgotten the different populations. You've got your plane enthusiasts and your train lovers. While people love to fly it's not the same as those who love to take the train.

Maybe you should schedule a ride for yourself, maybe on the Empire Builder or the California Zephyr. Don't tell anyone who you are, where you're going or what you're doing. Just put on a hooded sweatshirt, bring a book, wait outside along the train for the attendant to give you seat directions and blend in. Think anyone would recognize you?

It's probably been awhile since you've ridden coach, since you've kicked out the foot rest, leaned back in one of those reclining seats, and felt the gentle start and stop of the engine. It pulls away so easily, so quietly, you can't be sure you're moving. You have to look out the window to focus on a tree or a building. It's that smooth. Then you can remember why people take trains instead of planes. It's not always because they're afraid of flying. They just prefer the de-stress level. They don't like being treated like a commodity.

A couple weeks ago I rode the Texas Eagle from Dallas to Chicago. It wasn't the best start. It arrived three hours and twenty minutes late to Dallas from the West Coast. This kind of complicated my trip since I had two segments in front of me before getting back to Savannah. It messed up other people's schedules too, including a woman with very limited eyesight. We were sitting on the same wooden bench in Dallas. After we finally boarded I saw an attendant check on her and help her to the dining car multiple times. I thought that was nice.

She was cool about the delay. So was everyone else. We sat quietly in that beautiful downtown Dallas Beaux Arts station under 48-foot ceilings and original chandeliers (where 80 trains used to go in and out daily; what a sight that must have been) and here's the thing: no one seemed too put out.

The Texas Eagle, at 2,028 miles from beginning to end, is one of the longest routes in your company (my company, too, since Amtrak is a quasi-public corporation), so it's bound to be late with the mish-mash of freight trains. But that's another subject, right?

Cindi's, the deli across the street, helped ease the pain of waiting. I recommend the bagel and lox plate.

With the delay, I had time to visit the Sixth Floor Museum at Dealey Plaza, where on November 22, 1963, Lee Harvey Oswald crouched down behind a window to shoot President John F. Kennedy. The museum is a 10-minute walk from the train station, not so bad even if I did have to drag my suitcase. The museum, situated within the former Texas School Book Depository building, did a good job chronicling Kennedy's assassination and the historic times.

Later that evening, after the train finally arrived, I signed up for the 7:30 dinner reservation. These dining rooms run a strict show. Did you know that? You have to have a reservation and they hold to it. Lateness is discouraged. I find that interesting since trains themselves, well, you would have to say they are not very punctual.

That night, I shared a table in the Eagle's dining room with two brothers from Longview, Texas. They left Longview at 8:28 a.m. that morning, arriving in Dallas three hours later. Their tickets cost $28 each way. Maybe they got a senior discount. I forget. They came to visit the Sixth Floor Museum for the first time. They were cutting it close, but they planned to catch the 3:40 for their return trip home. When the train was late they decided to have dinner in the dining room. We were seated at the same table.

One of the brothers taught elementary school for many years and had just retired. The other brother writes for *Ride Texas*, a motorcycle magazine. As we waited for our main course, he told me he once rode his Harley-Davidson on

Highway 80 all the way from Texas to Tybee Island, outside Savannah, Georgia, my hometown. We laughed when I guessed where he had a beer once he dipped his toe into the Atlantic Ocean: The North Beach Grill, a friendly local place.

Another time he took a trip through the Ozark Mountains to Eureka Springs, Arkansas, on his Gold Wing motorcycle. We laughed again when I told him I used to live there, too. The world becomes very small and friendly when you start talking to people over dinner and, maybe, a drink. I've never had these kinds of conversations on a plane.

As we ate, there were pauses in the conversation, as if to imply the brothers were very familiar with one another; they didn't mind silence. They even ordered the same thing: Amtrak's "signature steak," a Black Angus flat iron steak with béarnaise sauce. It cost $25. They must be regulars on that train because the waiter asked, "Well-done, as usual?"

I ordered the butternut squash risotto with petite green beans and cherry tomato halves. The rigatoni pasta with oven-roasted tomatoes, mushrooms, peas and vegan soy sausage looked good, too.

Oh, but the snack bars. They could really use an upgrade, Mr. Anderson. I hit pay dirt on the Empire Builder and the Coast Starlight. They offered quinoa salad with black beans, corn, avocado and a chipotle-lime dressing. The other trains didn't even come close.

Once you board a train it doesn't take long to get comfortable and to see the lay of the land. Even before I made it to the dining car for my 7:30 reserved dinner seating, I checked out the sightseer lounge (using the exaggerated penguin step recommended by Victoria and others) to see what was happening.

That's when I saw Danny and his son, Tim. They were sitting next to one another, shoulder-to-shoulder on the same side of the table. They were watching a baseball game on a laptop, a light blanket thrown over their shoulders, a set of earplugs apiece. (Temperature control on the train might be something you could look into, Mr. Anderson. It's either really, really cold or really, really hot. That's a problem). Amtrak pins festooned their hats. They were tuned into an Oakland A's – Red Sox game while traveling from Tucson to Philadelphia, where they have family.

"Got a score on the Cubs' game?" I asked.

Danny said he'd check and get back to me.

After I finished my dinner I passed by on the way back to my seat. They were still there.

"Cubs ahead by two in the fourth," said Tim.

The dad is in real estate. He likes to unwind on the train. The son, 12, is a train freak.

"Always was," said Danny. "I hope he never outgrows it."

Then I noticed the scanner sitting on the table. I asked about it. Danny said they like to listen to the chatter between conductors and car attendants. Sometimes there's drama. In real time.

"Once they were throwing a guy off the train," Tim said. "I think he had a knife. We were riding through California, going through Donner Pass, and we listened to the cops chase him in the snowy road."

Note to self: Get one of the hand-held radio scanners. I wrote down the brand: A Radio Shack pro-649.

The next day I saw them again at the same table. Tim was watching another game.

That's when I saw a video camera he had attached to the window. He downloads what he shoots to YouTube. Most of it comes from the Sunset Limited, which passes their Tucson house three days a week. This interest started from a four-by-eight-feet train set Tim got as a kid.

"He even built a baseball field on it," his dad said. I checked out his video when I returned to my seat. Hundreds of people had viewed it.

Not everyone sitting in the sightseer lounge is that productive. Some people sit by themselves and look at the scenery: fields of sunflowers, piles of tires, backyards with trampolines and above-ground pools, barbecue grills, play sets, cemeteries, silos, sand piles, solar farms, random couches in the woods.

Nothing exciting, you might say. But in a world of sameness, of strip malls with your Dollar Store, Family Dollar and the occasional abandoned movie theater, small, local establishments are nice to see. Ned's Barber Shop, American Legion Post 13, Senka's Carpet, LV's Pub, KMK Insurance Co., Growden Heating, not to mention faded Coca-Cola signs on red brick buildings. They remind us we don't live in such a homogeneous world after all. Air travel can't do that. Neither can driving in a box on the highway.

Riding the train is a time warp. Between the nostalgia of the whistle and all the people I talked to who were no longer strangers, I felt very far away from Hurricane Irma and all its related disruptions, until I got a call from someone I live with in Savannah. She had decided to evacuate. She wanted to know what I wanted her to take of mine from the house. Passport? Photographs? Stashed cash? Art? That made the situation a little more real.

The effects of Irma got even more real when I received a text from Amtrak announcing the cancellation of the Silver Star. I was still in the Dallas station when I got this. It told me to call the "re-accommodation desk." That's an interesting term, don't you think? It seems the tracks carrying the No. 91 from D.C. to Savannah may have been compromised by the storm. Officials would have to check the viability before giving trains the go-ahead.

I understood the severity of the situation, but what I heard next did not please me. My choices, I learned, were slim. I could hang around Dallas, re-board the Texas Eagle and reschedule the D.C. – to – Savannah segment; I could ride to D.C., stay in a hotel for a few nights (at my expense) until the tracks were given the green light. Or I could fly back (or rent a car), at my expense. Whatever I chose had a deadline. I had to decide before boarding in Dallas. Maybe the tracks from D.C. would be approved by the time I got there. Maybe not. I had an hour to weigh the possibilities.

I caved. I booked a flight from Washington.

Danny, the real estate guy from Tucson, couldn't believe it when I told him my dilemma and then how I decided to fly back to Savannah.

"You did what?" he said, acting as if I had told him I was a member of the CIA and I had just turned him in as a suspect. I felt like a traitor for taking the plane, not the train.

I was still hopeful. While the airlines wouldn't give me a refund or make it easy to rebook, I could – if the tracks were fixed by the time we got there – redeem part of my cancelled flight. As soon as I got to Union Station in Washington, I checked the scheduling board. No dice. Number 91 to Savannah was cancelled. I had to fly.

After taking two long metro rides from Union Station to Reston, Virginia, I caught a connecting bus to Dulles International Airport, where I waited in a security line the length of the California coast to get on the plane. Then I transferred planes in Charlotte. I landed in Savannah four hours before the Silver Star would have arrived, had it been running.

Worse yet, there is no longer dining service on the Silver Star. That is sad. Such a pity. See what you can do about that, Mr. Anderson, OK? In the meantime, best of luck. We look for great things from you.

CHAPTER ELEVEN

FINDING POETRY, PHYSICS AND FARMERS ON THE CALIFORNIA ZEPHYR

A FEW YEARS BEFORE I TRAVELED on Amtrak's USA Rail Pass and became such a train zealot, I bought a one-way flight to California for a two-week stay at a friend's house in Big Sur. I planned on taking a train home. Since I wasn't sure how long I would stay I left my return trip open. When it came time to head back to Savannah I relied on "Julie."

Amtrak is very proud of its "Julie." She's patient, courteous, chipper. "Hi," the automated voice starts out. "Let's get started. You'll want a pen and paper handy." She is not afraid to admit if she doesn't understand something. She will say, "I'm sorry. I didn't get that." She's encouraging, offering "Got it" after every request. She's particular without being persnickety. She never loses her patience or raises her voice. She's a professional.

She doesn't quite have the humor thing down. She has not been programmed to understand or respond with irony.

"OK," the automated voice said when I dialed her up with a question. "You want to know the shortest route to Savannah from the Bay Area. Is that correct?"

I wanted to answer, "Well, I know it's kind of odd to ask for the 'shortest' route since Amtrak doesn't really specialize in short, right?" But she's not programmed to be cynical or questioning. She's not like a character in the movie *Her*, in which a lonely man (played by Joaquin Phoenix) develops a real-time relationship with a woman, an electronic operating system not unlike Julie. Spoiler alert: The relationship does not end well.

Still, Julie did her best with my request. I had flown to San Francisco, the closest airport to Big Sur, a rugged coastal town between Carmel and San Simeon, another destination that wasn't easy to get to without a car. There is no bus to Big Sur. From the San Francisco airport I caught BART (Bay Area Rapid Transit) to Oakland, then an AirTrain to Berkeley, where a friend had offered me a bed in her house. In the morning, we bicycled around Berkeley. I wanted to see Alice Waters' schoolyard of vegetables; I was not disappointed.

The next day I borrowed another friend's car that she leaves in Berkeley for when she's in town and nervously navigated the narrow, winding turns on the seaside cliffs of Route 101. I passed cherry farms, fields of garlic, strip malls, oil trucks, sea lions down below and lots of traffic. Later I was sorry I hadn't stopped at the Henry Miller Memorial Library in Big Sur, but the traffic had made me a little crazy. I still carry around Joan Didion's mental and written meanderings on the California freeways. She describes the driving as "secular communion." I hadn't arrived there yet. What she, a native Californian, called "a state of heightened awareness" I called fear.

Or maybe age.

I've always been a road warrior. Twelve-hour trips? No problem. Give me a book on tape and I'm there. Not so much anymore. Maybe it's the increased number of cars on the road, the humongous size of the trucks (and vans) or the ignorance of other people driving on the left when they should be on the right. I'm just not as patient or confident as I used to be.

After I maneuvered a challenging and steep dirt road to my place in Big Sur, I stayed put on top of a hill and enjoyed the sunsets, the anonymity, the unlimited days, the chance to work except for an occasional escape to the thermal hot baths at Esalen, *sans* clothing. I'm glad I did. That's where I met a group of "agrarian elders," rock stars of the sustainable food movement. They were meeting at Esalen to discuss the future of organic farming, which, they feared, was not promising. They and their aging cohorts had started to face reality: their children were not interested in carrying on what they had started. The average age of a farmer, I learned, is 57. From my corner in the hot springs I listened in on their conversations.

"I'm 72," one said. "I love what I do. But I can't keep doing it. Younger people don't have the resources or the knowledge. It's a real problem. That means there's no one to hand it down to."

I could appreciate their dilemma. Farming is hard work. But I had nothing to contribute. My only problem at the time was "talking" to Julie and finding a train back to Savannah.

At least Amtrak doesn't punish you with high fees for last-minute bookings. That would be a trick of the airlines. Except there is that problem of connectivity.

It's hard to believe that San Francisco – even with the highly successful BART for local travel – does not have an Amtrak station. Instead it provides a bus that takes you to nearby Emeryville, about ten miles across the bay in Oakland. It's a busy and fairly new station that sells Peet's coffee, hard-boiled eggs and a fine selection of books and magazines, something you don't find in most train stations. Usually, the best you can hope for is candy and chips from a machine.

The California Zephyr was my best bet. It starts its cross-country route in Emeryville and ends, as do most Amtrak routes, in Chicago. Then it would take two more connections before I could get back to Savannah. The whole thing would take eighty-eight hours. I would leave Emeryville on Wednesday morning at 9:10. Fifty-one hours later, in the same amount of time it took Diana Nyad to swim from Cuba to Miami Beach, the train would pull into Chicago on Friday afternoon at 2:40. That night I would catch the 6:40 Capitol Limited and arrive in Washington, D.C., at 1:05 the next afternoon. That left plenty of time to transfer to the Silver Star at 3:05. At 4:04 in the morning I would be back home in Savannah.

The California Zephyr wasn't always the only choice to cross the country from San Francisco, but it was since 2005, when Hurricane Katrina washed out the last section of the Sunset Limited, a route Amtrak does not intend to rebuild. The Southwest Chief, another option, leaves from Los Angeles.

After the Texas Eagle, the Zephyr is Amtrak's longest route. It runs 2,428 miles through California, Nevada, Utah, Colorado, Nebraska, Iowa and Illinois. It makes thirty-three stops.

"OK, folks, we're coming up to our first smoke break, in Truckee, California," said the burly, affable conductor.

For the beginning of the trip I was in the company of seven high school students from Seaside, a small town in northwestern Oregon. They were heading to the annual National Cowboy Poetry Gathering in Elko, Nevada, which started in 1983. I first caught a hint of this group when someone standing on the Sacramento tracks started reading a poem about reincarnation.

"You wrote this?" I said, impressed by its sentient nature.

"No," the girl said as if I were an idiot. "Wallace McRae did." She filled me in. "He's a rancher and a poet. We're going to see him at the festival."

Then someone started reading another poem. This one was original. It was about Mongolian cowboys. By this time the group had my complete attention. It turns out this poetry gathering is a pretty big deal. Maybe I should get off the train and go. My plans were fluid. I had the time. The headline speakers were Temple Grandin (whom I *had* heard of) and cowboy/poet Baxter Black, whom I used to hear regularly on NPR's Morning Edition.

"Forget trying to get in to see Black," someone told me. "He is so popular you would have had to submit your name to a lottery to even maybe be able to win a ticket. But I do have a ticket to see Ian Tyson, you know, from the duo Ian and Sylvia?"

Yes, I thought, dismissively. I've heard of Ian and Sylvia. I listened to them before you were born. Folk singers from Canada.

"He's 84," someone said. "Now he's a rancher."

Despite the warnings, I still considered getting out anyway at the 10 p.m. stop in Elko. In my experience you can always find a ticket to a concert or a play if you work hard enough. But where would I stay?

"There's no way you'll find a motel room," offered someone at the train's community-style dinner table. "I had to get mine months earlier." Plus, it was twelve degrees.

I would doubt my decision. For the rest of the day it nagged at me. Why am I always in such a hurry, which is completely nuts since I was taking a train, after all.

The next day, when a chatty conductor, Roger Wainwright, started his own poetic observations of what we were passing, I stopped doubting myself. I settled into the trip. This man, with a big belly, black suspenders and a conductor hat to match, had some age on him. He had personality.

"All right now," he started saying to anyone in the sightseer lounge car who would listen. "This is where we keep an eye out for wild mustang in the hills, right near that tumbleweed." I looked out the window but didn't see any. Someone else did, though. We were passing dramatic crevices formed by volcanoes in the Wasatch Range.

"One good storm and that's it for people who live here," he said. "I say, 'Thank you, Jesus, I live in Ogden, Utah.' Amtrak doesn't own any of these tracks. That's why we get stopped so much. Got to let the freight trains go first. Every time I ride through here, I look out the window and think, 'Ordinary people dug all this by hand.' It's really something."

By this time, Roger was gathering a crowd. We were still in Utah. "Now we have Thompson Springs, a dying town, a bitty town. At the last census they numbered 39. Supposed to be some Native American petroglyphs in caves. 'Thelma and Louise' was filmed there. Right there at the Silver Grill Café, known for its pies. All the place settings are still there. It was the home of a uranium boom in the late '40s, early '50s. Across from the Rio Grande depot."

Thelma and Louise, filmed in 1991. I loved that movie. The date sounded ancient. "Stop the train!" I said. "I want a better view!" Can't do that in a train. A car? Yes.

I didn't say anything about the millions of buffalo the train companies killed in their quest to reach the west – or the Native Americans that were displaced. It didn't seem the appropriate time.

The train was climbing. There'd be no stopping now. Hundreds of feet below we could see cars and big rigs on Interstate 80, "not a pretty sight after miles of forest and rock and rivers," Roger said.

He was right there. Still, I felt a little nervous.

"Now we're heading to Cisco," he continued, "another ghost town. At 3.25 percent grade for every hundred feet, it's got some of the steepest main lines in North America."

Roger's musings continued. People were listening.

"Interstate 70 and the demise of the steam locomotive killed the town. In the late 40s and early 50s there was a uranium boom there," he repeated for the people who were just getting on board with his musings. "At one time, two thousand people lived there. Now it's three. Uh oh, I feel another story coming on."

We were heading for Green River, Utah. It's the closest Amtrak stop to Arches National Park, except it's still fifty miles away. "You'd have to rent a car," Roger said, "but Enterprise closes at 5 and the train is supposed to get in at 4:10. Best to get off at the next stop. Grand Junction, Colorado. Look here. You can see the northern end of Arches National Park. It's large enough to fly a helicopter through. Rainbow Bridge is at the south side of Lake Powell. It's tall enough to fit the Washington Monument."

After Elko, the train stopped for about 30 minutes. "A coupler broke down and the freight train had trouble getting up the hill," Roger explained after talking on his walkie-talkie to the engineer. "That'll set us back. We pay Union Pacific to run our trains. They're making money hand over fist. They can afford to build more track, but there won't be any passenger trains as long as they can hire lobbyists to fight Amtrak."

Roger has been with the railroad 33 years. I wonder if they know what a treasure he is or if they hope he'll retire because he probably makes more money than younger conductors.

"Just because the train's stopped doesn't mean it's a smoke stop," he said. "The train in front of us went on emergency. We are waiting for it to be inspected. Thank you for your patience."

"Now we're passing the Colorado River," he continued. "It's frozen. Takes a lot to freeze it. This is Ruby Canyon. This is where we can see some mule deer. They have big antlers. Over-sized mule-like ears. There are some bald eagle nests, too. They like to spend the winter in the cottonwood trees."

He was on a roll.

"We ran over a bull once; every air hose we had was disconnected. The front of the locomotive was all bloody red."

After that bit of commentary from the loquacious Roger, I settled in at a table a little farther down the superliner observation car. Earlier I had spotted a young woman smart enough to bring her own snacks. She was reading *The*

Organic Farmer's Business Handbook by Richard Wiswall. Turns out she's an organic farmer in Maine.

"I majored in physics," she said. "I was on a pre-med track at Williams College. I thought, 'I'm gonna be a doctor and marry a farmer.' As a doctor I'd be telling people to eat good food. Then I realized I'd have to be in hospitals all day and I hate hospitals. So why not grow good food and come at it that way? Farming is my passion. So that's what I did. I became a farmer."

I couldn't believe my luck. I'm a gardener, an organic gardener and a would-be farmer – if I were forty years younger. She was the real deal. I hung onto every word. She's twenty-seven. I fell in love with her. I wanted to be her.

"It was hard to break the news to my parents," she said. "But they had read every one of Michael Pollan's books. That helped soften the blow.

"Equipment is a huge cost in getting started, so I have two draft horses. It's low-impact, horse-based farming. For compost I use crab shell." Green crabs, she said, are a menace on the Maine coast. "They compete with soft shell crabs."

She has a contract, "a guaranteed sale," with Mainers Feeding Mainers. This organization works in partnership with Good Shepherd Food Bank. Members include farms such as hers, dairies, fisheries and other local food producers aimed at eliminating hunger in Maine. Last year she grew five thousand pounds of produce on half an acre. They included rutabaga, beets, turnips and three thousand pounds of cabbage. Her farm is Helio Horsepower Farm in Bowdoinham, Maine, just north of Portland and Brunswick on the Kennebec River.

When she wasn't reading her handbook or ordering seeds from her catalogues, she spent her time knitting and flirting with a couple of Amish kids while their grandfather studied his Rot Druck or Luther Bible.

By this time I had started talking to a university professor who teaches physics and hates flying, which cracks me up since flying is all physics. He's from Cleveland and had taken the train to San Francisco to talk to some flutists about acoustics, frequencies and distances between blowholes, a subject that kept him up for hours. He's also a dog whisperer and a huge city of Cleveland enthusiast.

His ears perked up when the young farmer started talking about the Fibonacci pattern in the Veronica cauliflower she planned to order.

"It brings out the nerd in me," he said.

All I knew about the Fibonacci pattern I learned from Karen Foster, a potter friend from Eureka Springs, Arkansas. One year Karen took the petals in a sunflower and using Fibonacci maneuvered them into a stunning piece of art.

The professor and I were both riding coach, nodding off, catching a few winks when it got dark outside, getting off at the designated smoke breaks to stretch our legs or waiting for six a.m., when the snack bar started serving coffee. I told him the young farmer across the way had majored in physics. That's all he needed to hear.

"See? I told you," he said, turning to me. "Lots of people major in physics."

When the physicist talk got too technical I turned back to my book, James McBride's hilarious, *The Good Lord Bird*, something I picked up at a bookstore in Monterey, California. I liked McBride's earlier book, *The Color of Water*, and this newest one was short. He crafted a creative fiction approach to the John Brown abolitionist story that took place in Harper's Ferry, West Virginia. About fifty pages from the end, oblivious to the time or where I was, I looked out the window and saw where we had stopped: Harper's Ferry.

It wasn't physics but it was a coincidence. That's what can happen when you're riding a train.

CHAPTER TWELVE
LALA LAND

NEARLY TWO DAYS after we leave a dreary, damp Chicago, the Southwest Chief, known as the train of the stars, brakes to a near stop. We crawl the rest of the way into sunny Los Angeles' Union Station. We have traveled 2,264 miles through eight states, across the Mississippi River, alongside mountains, past deserts.

In 45 hours – two more than scheduled – we have reached LaLa Land.

"Look around, folks," our latest conductor announces. "Gather your belongings. This is the last stop on the Chief. Please don't forget your phone chargers. We have more than we know what to do with in our Lost and Found."

I say goodbye to my dinner mates from the night before, Sue and John from London. They thank me for the "smashing" good time we had together. I hope they weren't insulted by a story I told them about the time I was interviewing an Englishman. We were having breakfast and he ordered "a grit." I think from now on he'll know to order "grits." They were gobsmacked at the teeth of our newscasters – "Absolutely sparkling," John said – and blown away at the houses with trees and bushes planted in the front.

"I don't understand how Americans can do this," Sue said. "We would never do that. We need all the sunlight we can get. We wouldn't want to block any."

They love the royal family, "but not for what you may think," Sue said. "The fact is they bring in tourist dollars." I doubt I'll see them again. And that was fine. "Like ships passing in the night," said Sue, laughing lightly. She had just told me how they had traveled to America on the Queen Mary. She has problems with her ears. That's why she prefers trains (and boats) to planes. At our last breakfast together we shared stories of aches and pains. I showed her my crooked finger that just won't straighten out. I thought it was a volleyball injury, I said. Now I'm thinking arthritis. She complained about her bulging toe or hammertoe. I went on to my spondylolisthesis and my standing appointment with a chiropractor.

"Feet and ankles," she said. "They're just not as flexible as they used to be."

And with that, we parted.

Tuck away the winter jacket. Get out the sunglasses. I can feel the glam. Is this a movie set? Is this a cruise ship? Is someone really sitting at that upright piano in Los Angeles' Union Station, playing some show tune I can almost but not quite identify?

This would most likely be the same station my parents walked through on their honeymoon in the late thirties. That's a reach, thinking of them on a honeymoon. I wish I could have known them then. We three took such different paths in life.

The waiting room, commodious and bathed in ambient light, feels like the lobby of some glamorous hotel, a movie set or a luxury liner I've never taken. I pick up a brochure and learn about the station's Art Deco brass chandeliers, mahogany chairs, travertine walls. The architecture combines Spanish Colonial, Art Deco, Mission Revival. I look where I'm walking and see floors of terracotta tile and inlaid marble strips. Brass angels and sturdy ironwork surround 40-foot-high windows with original venetian blinds. Three-foot-tall wainscoting climbs the walls. Then I see hand-painted tiles, beamed ceilings and mahogany benches with worn leather seats.

I spot all of that before I step out into the courtyard and see orange trees, bougainvillea, fan palms, espalier magnolias. Be still, my heart. Out of curiosity, I check out a restaurant, one of many in the station. I am in a train station, right? For a second, I got confused. The painted floor in the restaurant looks like a Navajo blanket.

Despite similar architectural elements, this is not your ordinary Amtrak station. This is not the Amtrak the rest of us know or see. It has beauty but also function. Three dozen trains come in and out of this place a day.

It's a new day on a new coast.

Outside the station, teetering palms stand against the blue sky and the white stucco exterior. A clock on the facade displays the time. It's 10:00 in Tinseltown.

I cross the street, look for the No. 10 "Big Blue Bus," as instructed. There it is. I pay a dollar and climb aboard. I'm headed to an Airbnb in Santa Monica. My place sits next to the Artistic Center for Dentistry, an easy landmark.

What exactly does that mean? I didn't know, but somewhere between the light of the left coast and the lambent air I knew I was hungry. There are complete meals served in the Amtrak dining room, but they are limited. By the end of three days I was a little tired of the daily vegetarian special, good as it was, and not very interested in the featured flank steak. It would be a while before I again ate smoked almonds or yogurt, the best of the snack bar.

It was noonish so I walked to the first place I could spot with a crowd, Bay Cities Italian Deli and Bakery on Lincoln Boulevard. It was a good choice. While I waited for my pastrami, I asked the woman standing next to me if there was additional outdoor seating.

She asked where I was from (probably because I ordered the pastrami in an Italian deli, not the best choice). When I said Savannah, she swooned. She's from Chicago but she loves Savannah.

"But did you really take the train? All across the country? By yourself? I've never been on the train."

I told her she wasn't alone. Most people in this country haven't. Many people don't even know we have passenger trains.

"Anyway, I don't really have the time," she said. I felt as if she was implying her time is too precious to spend on a train. Or maybe I was being defensive about my age since I didn't have a steady job. But I moved on. More's the pity. I've put in my time in the workplace. Now it's your turn.

"I do," I said. "I have the time," although it hasn't always been something I could admit. "Having time" speaks of uselessness. It says you are without purpose, you are washed up. You're not even looking for a job. I used to hate it when people asked, "Are you retired?" But then I came up with a proper and pointed retort: "Writers never retire." I felt better with that answer at the ready. Let everyone else deal with changing schedules, pending raises, endless meetings, human resources, new bosses. I was free of all that.

But she was on to something else.

"If you're from Savannah you have to eat on the beach. It's only six blocks west."

"The beach?" I said. I hadn't thought of the beach. I was still on the train passing prairie dogs, going through tunnels, over mountains. I was peering down at rivers from bridges, counting cell towers. "Thanks. I will."

A little while later (after I paid 10 cents for a bag – the only one in line who did so – but I had to because of the creamy Italian dressing on the pastrami), she said, "Do you want me to take you?" I said sure. I am open to strangers; I trust my intuition. It turns out she was on a four-month break from her work. (Plenty of time to take the train somewhere, I thought).

She has one of those Hollywood jobs. She does awards publicity for Sony, figuring out strategy and logistics to get "product" screened. I told her I love that new use of the word "product," as if it were something manufactured, a bench, a table, something useful fashioned out of wood instead of "product" from a hair salon or a movie.

It wasn't so new to her.

I told her I didn't know one other person with her job. The world had changed. Move over, English teachers. I don't think I've met one for eons. Forget liberal arts. What does that even mean? Now people major in social media, corporate branding. Here in Los Angeles, people with those credentials flood the market.

The woman who operated my Airbnb was studying fashion Feng Shui. When I told her I was going to do a reading from my book, *The Dirt on Jane, an Anti-Memoir*, she asked my favorite colors, words, metals, fabrics. She wanted to know what I planned on wearing. She had already envisioned my book and my appearance as "product."

After a lot of dead-end answers, she decided I was a philosopher-type who would like flowy things (but not creamy Italian on pastrami). I wore what I brought, something simple. Probably red, my favorite color. She was disappointed. I told her I never knew anyone in fashion Feng Shui, but that I was sure she had a bright future. In the meantime, she has a temporary job. She babysits the children on the set of *Beverly Hills Nannies*. Everyone in Los Angeles has a temporary job.

After I ate my creamy pastrami sandwich on the very clean and very broad beach, I must have been thinking about fashion Feng Shui because I did a little shopping, which I never do. I went into what I thought must be a second-hand clothing store. The outside of the building was nothing special. The colors of the place were red and blue – nothing new there. I saw a group of svelte men and women dressed in black. They were setting up some kind of photo shoot. I ended up trying on a shirt that felt pretty good.

"This is nice," I said to the clerk. "I hardly ever find anything I like. I think I'll take it. By the way, how much is it?"

"It's on sale," she said. "Two hundred seventy-five dollars."

I said I would think about it.

When I tell my friend Sari that story, she roars. It's Fred Segal, high couture, she says. Never heard of it. Later I would eat sand dabs (sea urchins), learn about apriums, plouts and combinations of plums and apricots, and taste strawberry guava. Never heard of any of those either. I would get used to crossing the street while drivers waited for me ("It's the culture," my cousin Sheila explained), a generous habit that has since made its way to Slovannah, which is what we call Savannah.

I visited Phillippe The Original (over 100 years old), a diner close to Dodger Stadium that's been open since 1908 and waited in line to eat a French dipped sandwich. I would buy some of their mustard. I would learn it's almost cheaper to attend a play in Los Angeles than a movie, with a lot more of both to choose from. I would pass hedges of agapanthus, rosemary and lavender. I would meet a personal assistant of a famous movie star. One of her jobs? Twice a week, she has to brush the teeth of the star's dog. She didn't want me to say the star's name even though it's only a temporary job.

L.A. was grand. When I got home I regretted not buying that shirt, though I'm sure I would have spilled something on it the first wearing. I regretted not going to a Dodgers game. I never even checked the schedule.

Days later, after delivering a speech, I get back on the train for my trip east. But not before lunch with Sara, someone who lived in my old Detroit suburb way back when she was too young for me to pay much attention to though I adore her now. Not before good visits with cousin Sheila and her husband Michael. Sheila was one of those first-cousins who moved with her family to the West coast when she was very young. We were both good and competitive athletes. "You could run faster," she said, when we got together after some sixty years, "but I could jump higher."

I sat next to a woman who had taken the same train I took from Chicago. She's a retail buyer and had gone to Los Angeles to help open ten new Hudson Booksellers outlets the previous Monday morning. She lives in Montclair, N.J.

"All that matters is I'm there," she said when I ask about choosing to take the train over the plane. "The company doesn't care how I get there, if I decide to spend my weekends traveling." She has anxiety disorder, she said straight out, and doesn't like to fly. Never did. She'll get to Chicago, where she has a layover, go straight to a room she rents for four hours ("Seventy-five dollars"), bathe, change clothes and get back on the train.

"My husband commutes two hours each way to Brooklyn," she said. "He's a criminal defense attorney. That adds up, too."

She used to fly but it got to her. She faced blood pressure issues too. Because of all the flying she tried to quit her job. But then her company said she could take the train if that's what she wanted. So that's what she does – on the weekends.

We didn't sit next to each other long. Halfway to Chicago, she asked the conductor if there were any available sleepers. This is what experienced train riders do. Sometimes something opens up and you can get them for half-price. I thanked her for that tip, though I feel cramped in sleepers. I told her my only tips for riding the train were to wear a hoodie and bring an eye-mask, and a silver flask with something that goes down nice and warm and helps with sleeping. We both agreed Amtrak would be really smart to include a spa.

When my buyer friend from New Jersey got up for her sleeper, that left two seats for sprawling. They were good seats, too. Not too far but not too close to the bathroom. Double windows. My luck turned when two new people got on behind me. The first guy was fine. I didn't hear a peep out of him. By the time the second fellow arrived the train was full and he had to take that seat.

"You like Chinese food?" the first man started. Nothing wrong with asking that, although I thought it was a little random. Maybe he was just trying to be friendly, just making conversation. Except the syntax was weird so I peeked back between the seats. That's when I realized he was talking to a man from

China who didn't understand English. That didn't bother the American. He just kept on talking. When he wouldn't get an answer, his voice would get louder. He enunciated clearer as if that would do the trick. He tried everything. Either the man really didn't understand English or he just didn't want to talk to his seat partner.

"You like egg foo young?" he started. Hearing no answer, he continued with more food questions. "Chow mein? What about gong bao chicken?" He wouldn't stop. "Sweet and sour pork? Peking duck? Spring rolls?" I couldn't see the two but I felt as if I could hear the man who was Chinese shake his head in a bit of confusion.

The English-speaking traveler clearly uncomfortable with silence tried another tack. "You like basketball? You know tall player from China? Yao Ming. Very tall, extremely tall. Played for Houston." Then he went down another road. "You from Beijing? Shanghai?" When that didn't work he must have pulled out his phone because I could hear him speaking into some translation app that changed the English words into Chinese.

This went on for nearly an hour. Shoot me now, I thought. Because the train was not full I asked the car attendant if I could move. No problem, he said, removing the hand-written slip of paper from above my seat designating my final stop and moving me into the next car up.

The last I checked the American had given up and fallen asleep.

CHAPTER THIRTEEN

REFLUX, FLOSSING AND BALD SPOTS

AWOKE IN A PANIC, sometime after Albuquerque. After a long, dark stretch of track, I'd dozed off and was disoriented. This was unusual. Most of the time riding the train is pretty humdrum, but I'd had a bad dream. For a second I didn't know where I was. The sun sets early in January. The days are short. The book I was reading rested on my chest. I must have closed my eyes for a bit of a nap. Trains are good for naps, any time of day but especially late afternoon.

I was on the Southwest Chief, one of six Amtrak trains that cross the country east to west. The Chief runs daily between Chicago and Los Angeles, a distance of 2,256 miles. This was my second trip in three years on the Chief, which is how railroad folks describe it.

I had a new neighbor across the aisle and that was fine with me. The previous occupant, who boarded with me in Chicago the day before, had been listening to the Bible. He wore headphones. Still, the words bled through. I could hear every verse, every chapter. That was bad enough. Then he fell asleep. His head was bobbing. I thought about reaching over and pushing the "off" button. I could have reached it. I decided not to.

Later, he would pay me back for all my negative thoughts, even if he didn't know them. I had finally fallen asleep that night, despite the Bible recording, despite my nasty feelings toward Mr. Bibleman. Then someone's phone alarm woke me up. The same six tones beeped out, over and over again. I was livid. I got up, poked my ear closer to my Bible-reading neighbor, certain he or his phone was the perpetrator. Nope. I tried the person in front of me. Not her. I walked closer to the man behind me. Not him either. I sat down exasperated, spent. That's when I saw the blinking. That's when I knew whose phone alarm was making the racket. It was mine, tucked in the webbing on the back of the seat in front of my knees. Payback. Did anyone on Car 12 of the Southwest Chief see me grab the phone and turn it off? Hope not.

In Winslow, Arizona, my nemesis got off and my new neighbor got on.

He popped open his laptop as soon as he sat down. He kept his eyes glued on the screen. I was grateful. Sometimes you want company; sometimes you don't. After that his fingers started tapping on his keyboard. Later we would talk. I would learn he's a researcher in chemistry. He was inputting data. He had been out to Chicago to present a paper, stopped along the way in Winslow to visit his children. A little while later, either he started singing or it was in my mind, but I began to hear that Eagles song about a girl, a flatbed, a corner, a Ford.

"Why did you have to sing that?" I said, playing with him a bit, speaking my thoughts as is my wont. With age, I was learning, there is no filter. We tend to say anything that pops into our head. "Now that song about Winslow is stuck in my brain."

He was headed back to Los Angeles. He liked the train; it gave him space to think, to work. I told him I was working on a book about Sandy West, a bold, imaginative woman who fought to keep Ossabaw Island wild and free of development. Ossabaw is one of a series of barrier islands off Savannah. Sandy's still alive. She's 106. Before I boarded the train, someone told me how Sandy, who was born Eleanor, acquired her name. It was on a train. She was traveling with her sister-in-law, Elizabeth Pool, when they encountered an inebriated passenger. He renamed them Sandy and Rusty. Sandy does have light-colored hair. Elizabeth Pool, who co-wrote *God of the Hinge: Sojourns in Cloud Cuckoo Land* with Sandy, was a redhead.

In my seat I was shuffling paper, drawing arrows, using a red marker. I had a lot to fit together.

That's when he looked up and said, "Old school, eh?"

I looked up, surprised someone was talking to me. Unless you're in the observation car, where chairs are riveted to the ground and can swivel, where fixed windows arch up and around from the floor, where conversation is encouraged and common, no one talks too much between aisles. It's like there's a code or something. But here it was: someone talking to me.

"Old school?" I said, looking at the pile of papers. "I guess so. It works for me."

We turned back to our projects. Maybe an hour later we both got up, almost at the same time. There are no seatbelts on trains – something I don't quite understand – so it's possible, though not always easy, to just stand. We both had the same idea. Time for the sightseer lounge. He followed me. We took seats across from one another at a table, a four-top, squeezing into the bench.

"Never groan when you get up or down from a couch," he blurted out. "Sophia Loren said that."

"Good one," I said. "Do you know how many people have never heard of Sophia Loren?"

"Pity."

That's when I knew I had found a compatriot. It's so hard these days, on or off a train. Not that I mind young people. I don't. They're fresh. They have energy. They're smart, even if they never heard of Rachel Carson or the Kinsey Reports. They can fix my electronics. Still, there are gaps. As I have often told them, "I have t-shirts older than you."

One day, when I used to visit my mother in her assisted-living facility in Southfield, Michigan, where the aides were always gossiping, one of my favorites nudged me at breakfast. She bent over and whispered, "Diana Ross' father just moved in down the hall from your mom. He's over there, that tall, light-skinned, good-looking black man in the wheelchair."

When another aide, anxious for any kind of distraction, heard that she said, "Who's Diana Ross?" The first aide rolled her eyes. "She's Tracee Ellis Ross's mother." That's when I said, "Who's Tracee Ellis Ross?" Now I know. She's an actress.

Except for the variety of ages, trains are sort of like assisted-living residences, especially on long-distance rides. People trade in gossip. They look for diversion. You talk to people. If you want to. You open up to strangers. If you want to. You say what you want, knowing you'll never see these people again. It's easy. Time and sociability take on different dimensions.

We sat at the table, my neighbor across the aisle and I, next to the windows, happy to stretch, happy to be out of our seats for a while, happy to be watching the country, albeit in the dark, roll by. We did have some moonlight. We passed barns covered with snow, cows, fields of brown grass poking through, the skeletal remains of tractors. Neither of us felt the need to talk. After ten minutes or so of silence, my new friend, keeping his eyes turned to the window, said, "I have reflux."

Without questioning this out-of-the-blue announcement, I offered a knowing, sympathetic nod. Everyone I know these days seems to have reflux.

"What did we used to call these things before doctors or drug companies gave them names?" I said.

He just shook his head. No answer. There was no answer.

The conductor walked by, his ring of keys jangling, a passel of papers in his hands.

"We'll be stopping for a few minutes, folks," he said. "Nothing to worry about. A cow is on the tracks. You can't hurry a cow, can you? We're working on getting him up and outta there."

"I have vertigo," I said, picking up where we left off.

He nodded before returning to his state of reflux. "I try not to eat before going to bed," he said. "Then there's tonight when I'll probably mess everything up."

That reminded me of the stretchy exercise band I'm supposed to be using for a wonky knee. I broke it when I tripped on some construction wire walking in Tel Aviv. Except I forgot to bring it. There's no room for that on a train, anyway, I rationalize. But who am I kidding? I tell him something I've never told anyone: "I've never used it. Never even taken it out of the plastic wrapper. Ridiculous, I know."

At least one friend never lets me live down that trip or that accident.

"I told you Israel was dangerous," Billy said.

I move on to something else. "I am stocking up on hydrogen peroxide for the vertigo. For when it happens again. Peroxide breaks up the otoliths. That's what causes the vertigo. They may sound Russian, but they're these little calcium deposits that get stuck in the curve of your ear canal."

"My mom used peroxide for everything," he said. "Vinegar, too. She loved vinegar. It cleans scissors. Window blinds, too."

Just as the train pulled in to Kingman, Arizona, we moved on to teeth.

He said he's had four dental implants and is wearing a bridge while he waits for the gum to grow over the screw so he can get a fifth implant. He hates taking the temporary bridge in and out to clean, although after all the appointments – to say nothing about the money – he's reconsidering the bridge thing.

I've had three implants. I know what he's talking about. "Don't you hate it when a tooth next to the implant gets a cavity and they have to mess with that too?" I ask. "Not fair."

Implants must be in the air because the next day one of the Amish gents, unusually talkative, told me he and his crew were heading to a clinic in Mexico. He was going to get a dental transplant. Much cheaper there, he said.

That same day, in the observation car, I started talking to another Amish couple. The children were playing Bible Bingo. They were from Indiana. They, too, were traveling on dental business. "The missus had dental transplant surgery in Tijuana, Mexico," her husband said. "We got off in San Diego, walked across the street to the commuter train, caught the blue line and got off in San Ysidro at the Mexican border. Then we walked up with our passports – and a big smile – to the immigration office, passed through and took a taxi to the dentist's office. Someone told us to always smile."

They were there in a hotel for one week. The first night was free. The dentist pulled all her teeth and prepped her for two implants. That was two months ago. They're going back for a return checkup.

I didn't tell him one of my implants had just broken. Metal fatigue, my dentist said. It happens. He tried probing, to pull out the seat so he could re-screw it. I said I had a Phillips screwdriver in my car if that would help. He didn't laugh. After a while he turned off his drill, took off his magnifying glasses, leaned back in his seat and said, "How've you been doing chewing?"

"That question is not a good sign," I said.

He couldn't retrieve the seat in my gum. To repair the implant I would have to have surgery to extract and replace.

"I wouldn't do it," he said. "And at your age …"

"How old are you?" I asked.

"Sixty-three."

A point well taken.

"I am 75," I said. "I am chewing just fine."

Later I changed my mind and returned to my other dentist who did retrieve the screw. Maybe it was the bumper sticker I gave him: "Don't Drill." He loved it. The phrase comes from One Hundred Miles, a nonprofit environmental organization dedicated to protecting the Georgia coast. Did I ever think I'd have two dentists?

The Amish don't like to fly. It's too fast-paced. This couple told me they run a general store. They put all their expenses on an Amtrak credit card – "See?" he said, holding up the card – and then travel on points. They seemed to be traveling with nine or ten friends.

I'm glad my aisle mate and I got so personal about health issues. Now he'll understand all the picking and flossing I've been doing. The train is great for many things but not for the bathrooms, where it's in and out, quick, quick, quick. People are waiting. Flossing has to be done from the seat, looking out the window.

The conductor was right. Fifteen minutes later the cow picked itself up and moved across the tracks. We were up and going.

"On the other hand," my new best friend said, "did you know gray hair is trending?"

I did not expect to hear the term "trending" from him. He's a scientist with very short hair. He's not a guy who looked particularly vain. I kept that to myself. Then he told me a story.

"When I was young I had this long, long hair," he said. "I dyed it purple, all kind of colors. I was in a club one night. I went to the john and there were all these mirrors. On my way out I caught a glimpse of someone with a bald spot and I thought, 'That's funny. I thought I was the only one in here.' It was me. I was the one with the bald spot. I went out and really laid into my friends. I said, 'How come you didn't tell me?' That's when I started cutting it short. See? See my bald spot?"

"Even Rafael Nadal has a bald spot," I said. "Same with Tiger Woods."

Men and male pattern baldness. It's a thing.

Then I told him a story about me and gray hair.

"I used to think it was my hair that tipped people off to my age," I started. "But last year I was riding the subway in New York, holding on kind of awkwardly to one of those handle loops hanging from the ceiling, swaying back and forth with the jerk of the train, trying to be cool. I was wearing a crazy wool giant hat that made my hair look like it was cut in a Mohawk. I bought it on the street the day before for $5 because the wind had picked up and it was so darn cold. You know how that happens in New York.

"I know for a fact none of my hair was showing when we got on the subway. Not one bit. Still, someone very politely offered me a seat – and he called me 'ma'am.' I'm used to 'ma'am' because I live in Savannah, but in New York? That really bummed me out. That's when I realized it was not the hair that gave me away. It was the face, my face. It's old. What are you going to do?"

CHAPTER FOURTEEN
REGRETS IN MALVERN

WHEN THE TEXAS EAGLE finally pulled into the station at Malvern, Arkansas, at 3:55 a.m. – right on time – I realized my mistake. It was lunacy, really. I come from the school of don't-overthink-stuff. That's where you put yourself out there, sometimes on a limb, and see what you can do. Some people seek thrills by climbing mountains or swinging on a zipline. I take trains, which can mean buses too.

Sometimes the less you know the better you are. This time I might have pushed my luck too far. For this trip, I patched together a flight from Savannah to New York City with a friend, a teacher who had limited travel time. From NYC, I decided I would only take trains to get to my final destination – a wedding in Eureka Springs, Arkansas – *even if* it meant going to Chicago to catch a train to Malvern, Arkansas (the closest Amtrak station to Eureka, some 220 miles away), then transferring on and off three buses to the little Ozark mountain town in northwest Arkansas.

No one said it was easy to travel by train.

My old friend Dina's son, Favio, was getting married. Dina and I met in Eureka in 1976. I didn't want to miss his wedding.

On Monday, when my friend headed off on the F train to New York's LaGuardia Airport, I wheeled my suitcase down Seventh Avenue to Pennsylvania Station in plenty of time to catch the Capitol Limited.

Because there is no direct route to Arkansas, I thought I would stop in Chicago overnight to visit my friends Nicole and Janice. Then I would board the Texas Eagle headed to Malvern. No one in Eureka Springs – or anywhere – had ever heard of Malvern.

"It's the brick capital of the world," I toss out, certain there must be something singular about the town.

Amtrak makes only three stops a day in the whole state of Arkansas, one more than in Tennessee. None of them are very convenient. I learned this from a seatmate in coach. She lives in Nashville.

"We have no service at all," she sighed.

Malvern seemed the best bet. Billy Bob Thornton went to high school there. That should count for something.

But first I had to get from New York to Chicago. There were several routes I could have chosen. I picked the Capitol Limited, a route I always seem to end up on. The 959-mile trip would take twenty hours. After a pleasant three-hour ride passing along the Potomac Valley, we stopped in Albany to change from electric to diesel. Amtrak officials called it a smoke stop. But really it was a chance to pick up four or five more cars. We also picked up a couple in their eighties who had ridden their bikes from Vancouver to Albany. They were headed for Cleveland, but after all that riding they didn't seem anxious to talk; they made a beeline for the sleeper car.

That night, in the train's culture of seating people community style, I learned my dinner partner was from Buffalo. He works at the Buffalo Fine Arts Academy but was born in Bangladesh. In the confusion of the day (that's my excuse anyway), I was embarrassed to admit I couldn't place Bangladesh. He didn't seem to mind. Bangladesh sits east of India, he said. Most of his relatives moved to Toronto. He told me to look him up if I were ever in the museum in Buffalo. He would give me a tour.

"If you forget my name, just ask for the brown man," he said lightly.

I would choose the same dinner four more times in the next two weeks – the "healthy option," in this case Asian noodles. For $16 it did the trick, that and a Scotch on the rocks.

"A double?" the black-and-white suited waiter asked

"Sure, why not?"

I slept well that night, as I usually do in coach, especially with Scotch or Bourbon, especially when the seat next to me is empty. When dawn broke, I looked out and saw hundreds of wind turbines in northern Ohio. Aside from a woman across the aisle who was talking to her sister, ("Hello? Are they at the funeral home yet? Is Aunt Bee there? Hey, Granny Baby, it's me"), the car was quiet. We pulled into Chicago on time at 9:45 in the morning. I detrained, crossed on foot over a bridge on the Chicago River, walked down to South Wabash Avenue, climbed up one flight of iron stairs and took the Brown Line (formerly the Ravenswood). I passed my old street (Armitage Avenue) and got off at Southport, where Nicole and Janice met me in time for lunch.

The next afternoon I got on the 1:45 Texas Eagle, Number 21, for Malvern. For a while, we paralleled Interstate 55. I felt oddly smug, clearly giddy not to be stuck in automobile traffic. I pushed back my seat – more like a living room recliner or a Barcalounger – kicked out the foot rest, laid the book I intended to read on my chest and stared out the slightly tinted window, amazed again how gently trains start and stop. There is no jerking. I was very happy not to be driving.

At seventy-nine miles an hour, time was starting to flatten out. We passed fields of sunflowers, piles of tires, backyard trampolines, above-ground pools, cell towers, water towers, silos, sand piles, random couches in the woods. Around 7:30 p.m., just as the sun started to set, we crossed the Mississippi River and approached St. Louis; the six hundred thirty-foot Gateway Arch loomed in the distance with Busch Stadium nearby.

At dinner I sat with a couple of proud St. Louis folks who told me, "No building in St. Louis can be taller than the Arch."

They volunteer at the botanical gardens, "the third best in the world," she said.

"Come sometime, I'll show you around."

Again, someone was offering to give me a tour.

"We're spoiled in St. Louis," she said. "Our zoo and art museum are free. We went to the art museum in Chicago. It cost $29 to get in."

Midwesterners: they're so friendly, so optimistic. You have to look hard to find any guile.

When I tucked back into my seat by the window, with my University of Michigan hoodie pulled down over my eyes, the cord tied tight, I considered the exorbitant $175 sweatshirt I almost bought at the new Whitney Museum of Art in New York. That's what credit cards will do. It was a done deal until I noticed this beautiful piece of apparel did not have a draw cord around the hoodie. Forget it! I bought a postcard instead.

After dinner I started to worry the attendant wouldn't wake me up. In typical low-tech Amtrak-style when the conductor saw my ticket, he slipped a piece of scrap paper above my seat with the words "MAL" (short for Malvern) on it. I didn't see anyone else in my car with the same designation. This was supposed to remind him to wake me up.

I still wasn't sure how I would get from the train depot in Malvern to the bus station that would take me to Eureka Springs. But how hard could it be? I would wing it. The Texas Eagle comes with a miserable on-time performance figure – fifty-seven percent – so maybe the train would pull late into Malvern and I wouldn't have so long to wait for the bus. The bus was scheduled to leave at 8:30. The good news is I was traveling alone so I didn't have to worry about anyone else's fears or anxieties. I could set the tone and make my own mistakes.

As timing would have it, the attendant didn't have to alert me. I slept fitfully, afraid he'd forget to wake me, afraid I'd miss my stop. He came by at 4 a.m. I gathered my stuff, walked down to the detraining area and stood there next to one other person.

"Say, think I could grab a ride into town?" I asked, thinking this might be my ticket into Malvern.

Wrong. She didn't have a car. Her boyfriend was meeting her. She did not pick up the hint and offer me the desired ride. The train pulled away – they don't tarry – and there we stood, the two of us, in an open courtyard with crushed cigarettes, a plastic water bottle, a used condom and some graffiti scratched on the concrete wall: "Amtrak can suck my dick."

My initial reading in Wikipedia of Amtrak's Malvern station promised a "Mediterranean Revival style" station, a red brick building constructed in 1916. This was the brick capital of the world. But that is not what I found. That is not what Amtrak is using for its one-a-day train. The historic building sat across the tracks. The two of us stood there for a while in silence. It was awkward. She still hadn't offered me a ride but I had hope. She lit a cigarette. I should initiate some conversation, I thought. She beat me to it.

"You'd think if we hadn't seen each other in two weeks he'd be here," she said.

"How long have you been together?"

"Ten years. I was headed to Houston to work after the hurricane, to make some money. But I didn't have my ID. He was supposed to bring it. He never showed."

"What do you think happened?"

"It's a long story."

"You want to walk into town while you tell me?"

We headed up the hill into the darkness of Malvern, my suitcase bumbling along after me. Then I noticed the funny way she was walking.

"What happened to your leg?"

"I was born without a knee." Pause. But that was it for the knee. "That little fucker. He's not coming."

"What do you think happened?" I asked again.

"He was in a psych hospital last week just after I left. He tried to shoot himself. But I know he's out. He called me."

We kept walking. She started to cry. She had lost her phone in Houston in the Hurricane Harvey clean-up operation, where she couldn't get a job because she didn't have any ID. That was the ID he was supposed to bring for work. She was staying with her boyfriend's sister in Malvern, but even if she did have a phone the sister worked overnight so my travel mate didn't want to call and wake her up.

"Do we have much further to go?"

"There's a McDonald's up ahead."

We passed the shuttered-up town until we got to the yellow arches, which I was grateful to see. She sat on the curb, lit another cigarette, and I went inside. They were just setting up for the day. No one could find the drawer of change. When I came back out with a cup of coffee for her, she was gone. Then I went back inside. I needed to find the bus station – or Keeney's. This is a grocery store I had read about that serves breakfast starting at seven. It sits in the middle of an old neighborhood. I still had time before my bus. The place got rave reviews on Yelp. Once again I thought, "How hard could it be to find?"

"Keeney's?" said the second customer of the day. "It's got great ribs. Not too far from here. Turn left at the light, keep walking 'til you see the school, then head right. Can't miss it. I'd go with you but I'm here tending my little sister.

She just got out of rehab or a psych hospital. Same thing. We're in the motel across the road. I don't want to leave her too long."

"Can't miss it," the guy behind the counter said. I headed out, dragging my suitcase in the dark, grateful once again for wheels. I cut across the parking lot of a tractor supply company, passed a muffler/transmission place, then an auto garage, a pawn shop and another pawn shop. This one sold guns. Traffic was light, and it was still dark. There were no sidewalks, only patches of grass, rocks, glass, uneven pieces of concrete curbing. Traversing was tough. I was starting to have second thoughts about Keeney's. When a yellow dog with yellow eyes and white teeth lunged out at me at the end of a long leash attached to a tree I got scared. I turned around and headed back to McDonald's.

"Bus station?" the kid behind the counter said, repeating my question. "You can't miss it. Turn right at the light, cross the overpass – you'll see the railroad tracks below – and keep walking."

I started out, a little less certain than before. My confidence was flagging. I tried sticking out my thumb to hitch a ride. Maybe someone will feel sorry for me and pick me up. No one did. I stopped at a Medlink Medical transport company off the highway to confirm the directions. Then I asked if he wouldn't mind taking me. They're supposed to serve the public, right? He would mind. He wasn't allowed to.

I thought about playing the "old" card. If not now, then when? But I didn't.

I started out again. Traffic grew heavier as the day brightened; what I was doing started to feel dicey. I crossed four lanes of traffic in haste, turned where he told me to on West Moline Street and finally saw a young girl carrying a school flag. Yes, she confirmed. The bus station is straight ahead. The doors were closed but a young woman was sitting on a bench under a kiosk waiting for the same bus. She was heading to Fayetteville, near Eureka Springs, to relieve her sister who had been taking care of their mother. "She just got out of rehab," the woman said.

Two bus connections later, waiting in yawning stations with low ceilings and televisions blaring news of Hurricane Irma, I sat on the bench among a woman nursing a baby, another woman holding two bulging black plastic garbage bags and a man clearly just out of prison. He was wearing a pair of white sneakers and some pressed khaki pants. He was holding a Bible.

Besides the coffee at McDonald's and a package of peanuts from the Kum & Go convenience store I had had nothing to eat all day. I was feeling a bit peckish, irritable. Doubt started to creep in. What a stupid idea this was. Then my mind circled back to the woman with no knee, no phone, no place to stay, no boyfriend, no one to call, no ID. She had so little. I had so much. Two days earlier I had nearly spent $175 on a sweatshirt I saw at the Whitney in New York. Why didn't I offer to help her more? Why didn't I give her some money? I wish I had.

CHAPTER FIFTEEN
O CANADA, O CANADA

HOURS BEFORE I LEAVE for Canada I remember my passport. I need to pack my passport. It's a stretch to think of Canada as a foreign country. They look like us. Most of them talk like us. They laugh like us. They're not like us. For starters, they travel. Sixty percent of Canadians have passports. In the U.S., it's 36 percent. In Great Britain and Australia, it jumps to 75 percent.

After a visit with my cousin Maggie in Gibsons, on Vancouver's Sunshine Coast, I planned to take a train from Vancouver to Toronto. In four days and four nights I would cross two time zones and five provinces: British Columbia, the prairies (Alberta, Saskatchewan and Manitoba) and Ontario. I would show my passport when I entered and left Canada.

From Gibsons, I took the 6:20 a.m. BC ferry across Horseshoe Bay, the 257 Horseshoe Bay express bus to downtown Vancouver, and then a city metro to catch the train. The connections couldn't have been simpler. Plus, it was Sunday: so much easier to see the bones of a city without traffic. I got off the bus at the cream-colored terra cotta Hudson's Bay Company department store in front of a couple of massive Corinthian columns and a flyer stapled to a utility pole: "Premium marijuana delivered to your door in 60 minutes, free delivery."

The city's nearby SkyTrain drops you off a block from Pacific Central, another elegant Beaux Arts beauty in neoclassical revival style, another reminder of how popular and important train travel used to be.

The depot was one location you really couldn't miss. The name Pacific Central stretches across the top of the building in oversized orange letters. Nothing was open when I arrived. With the help of two young women from Sweden who were on holiday I finally found Wi-Fi in a small A&W restaurant tucked in the corner of the station. A&W, a throwback of a brand, was founded in 1919, the same year the station was built. The women were getting off in Jasper, a popular and scenic mountain town about twenty hours away. Their English was perfect.

I intended to sleep in coach (they call it economy class in Canada), but after so many people recoiled at the idea of curling up like a shrimp for all that time I thought I'd check on the price of a sleeper. It would be $2,943 for four nights. Unless you travel on a Tuesday. Tuesday is bargain day. Too late for that and way too expensive, even if the ticket does include three meals a day and the dining room does sport real cutlery, porcelain plates and some fancy chandeliers. I'll do that another time, I thought, maybe when I'm old, really old.

If I expected a big difference between Amtrak and Canadian rails, I didn't find it – unlike in Spain, where the electric train from Seville to Barcelona, for instance, hums along at 176 miles an hour, information that is presented on a computer screen in each car, along with the expected time of arrival.

In Spain, it's trucks, not trains, that carry most of the freight.

Not so in Canada. There, we experienced the same delays Amtrak faces. In both countries, freight companies own the tracks. They call the shots. None of it mattered to me. I wasn't in any hurry except when we left Manitoba for Ontario and I started to worry about making my 10 p.m. flight back to Savannah. That's when I heard we were some five hours late. I didn't need to worry. We made up the time. We pulled into Toronto 20 minutes late.

One time I looked up and counted a train carrying nearly 200 intermodal shipping containers, stacked double. And I didn't even start counting at the beginning. That's a lot of freight going between Vancouver and Toronto, lots of stuff coming in from China, I'm sure, and lots of wheat, canola and potash leaving Canada.

"We're the bread basket of the world," Jeremy, a friendly car attendant, said. "But with 35 million people we can only eat so much bread. If the price of wheat is down, farmers store the grain near the tracks until winter. That's another story," he said, "taking the train in the winter. But we're ready. We have giant snow plows on the engines and plenty of propane to melt the ice."

On neither the Canadian transcontinental passenger train nor Amtrak are you assigned a seat. In both instances, it's just, "Toronto? The car to the right," or "Saskatoon? To the left." The rest is up to you. I like to look for a double window that extends into the seat in front of me for unobstructed views, somewhere in the middle, away from the bathrooms.

Other than that, finding compatible neighbors is a crap shoot. With four days and four nights in front of me, I needed some luck. I found it. My nearest neighbor was Mark, an Australian with a gray handlebar mustache and warm brown eyes. He knew when to talk, when not to talk. When he saw me look across the aisle, eyeing his creative sleeping arrangement, he got up and helped me hook the footrest of the empty seat next to me to the pull-down tray on the seat in front. This created the desired flat surface for stretching out. He would do that every night.

Later I learned Mark's wife had died four months earlier. After her death, he thought about staying home but figured it'd be best to take the trip they both had talked about. His eyes teared up when he told me that. He wasn't the first widower I met on my trains. As a kid, he always thought he'd be a "train driver" but the profession he did choose – nursing – turned out to be a much better fit for him. It's less lonely than sitting at the wheel, he said.

Every morning he would catch my eye and ask softly, "Did you sleep well?"

There's no modesty in coach class. Neither of us looked our best. I was so unprepared for the cool evenings in my August trip, I resorted to wrapping a long, soft, sleeveless red dress around my neck as a scarf. I fished out two long-sleeved shirts from my suitcase. For the whole trip I wore them on top of two short-sleeved shirts. For a pillow, I wrapped the rest of my clothes as best I could into a ball. Smart people brought blankets but I like to travel light. That does not include a blanket.

Smart people also bring their own food. I try but it never works. I've got a bad habit of eating everything I have within a few hours. This time cousin Maggie sent me off with topnotch chicken, steak, hummus and flourless chocolate cake. It lasted half a day.

There are some perks to buying food on the Canadian. It's good. You order and pay at a take-out area right off a narrow aisle next to a window. If someone is trying to pass by, you practically squeeze into the kitchen. The order goes directly next door to a chef in a small kitchen visible to all. Everything is cooked to order. There's no tableside service. When your order is ready he or she calls your name. Credit card, American cash, Canadian loonies and toonies are all accepted.

When a woman traveling with two children had only a debit card, Jeremy called ahead to the next station to see if it had an ATM.

"They have one," he said. "The problem is we won't be there long enough for you to access it. I'm sure the cook will let you run a tab."

Very trusting, these Canadians. Very thoughtful.

The down side to this system is there is no community seating as in Amtrak (and the tony Canadian sleeper cars). Yes, you can take your meal and sit with a stranger, someone you may not normally talk to, but no one does. Most times you end up eating alone. My last night on the train my new friend Wendy, from Vermont, invited me to sit with her and her husband, Al. He's a wood turner. They chose salmon. Since I had eaten that the past two nights I went for the pot roast. They had just come off a 25-day canoe trip into the bush with four friends. I saw them in their seats spreading out a map of everywhere they went. They were all over 65.

When they finished their trip, they had a plan to meet the train by the side of the tracks in what is known as a flag station in a small house owned by someone from an indigenous family.

"Probably Ojibwa," said Wendy.

The train was three hours late. They ended up sitting on their luggage, with their canoes, cook stove, tents, gear nearby. They showed me a photo they took waiting for the train. Wendy is standing in the middle of the tracks, trimming Al's beard, somewhere in Ottawa.

I met the canoeists at what seemed to be an impromptu afternoon concert in the lounge area. VIA Royal, Canada's passenger rail service, has an Artists on Board program. The company covers the travel expenses of the singer in exchange for three mini-concerts a day. It was a nice diversion. He sang tunes by Al Green, John Lennon and then a new singer/songwriter favorite, Sam Amidon.

"We know of him," Wendy said. "He's from Vermont."

It's a casual concert. While a Canadian mayor from some small town and his two sons raised their cans of Orange Crush in a toast to their trip, a couple of kids played Rock Paper Scissors – which seems to be making a comeback – followed by Scrabble. A young mother changed her baby's nappy.

Trains seem to be good venues for kids. They can walk (or run) around. But while I like children, listening to their mother or someone else try to control them mile after mile gets a bit tedious. "Do you have to go potty?" "Don't jump on the seats." "You stay here." "Granny says no." "Didn't you bring some kind of screen in your bag? No? Well sit down on your bum." "Granny's getting tired." By now I know they will fall asleep eventually, so I try to be patient.

We can walk around, too. If you're not happy in your seat you can always walk to the quasi-café or climb some steps to the Dome, the glassed-in, elevated space above the dining area. There are plenty of social opportunities, but unlike at a cocktail party where you might feel trapped in conversation, on a train you have options. You merely retreat to your comfort zone of a seat. It's a cocoon and it's yours. No one else's.

One early morning when I couldn't sleep I made my way up to the Dome in time, quite by accident, to see the sun rise. We were in the Prairies, a vast area of nearly 780 square miles of plains, forest and farmland. That's when I met Barbara. She likes to sleep up there. Barbara's an air traffic controller in Tijuana. She likes to counter her time with tense airline passengers with days on the train. She said she spends a month and a half of her salary every year taking the train. This time she took Amtrak up the coast of California to Vancouver. She planned to meet her son in Winnipeg.

As she was telling me this, Jeremy, who writes and reads dystopian novels in his spare time on the train, came up and announced, "A minute and a half until sunrise."

Then the train stopped.

"What's happening?" I asked. "I don't see a freight train."

"Crew change," he said. "Twelve hours on, then it's hand off."

"But how will anyone find us?" I asked, looking out at a vista of green.

"Oh, they will."

That's when I spotted a couple of headlights snaking through the dark fields. Minutes later I saw the car door open and a man in an orange fluorescent jacket get out of the car. Our new conductor.

Usually I could spend hours with the scenery as company. But this was the end of my trip and I was thinking of home. I started to feel antsy. While I could charge my phone at my seat, there was no Wi-Fi service.

"Nice, isn't it?" I said to my neighbor Mark, trying to talk myself into it.

But I really didn't think so. And I never really believed it. I kept trying again and again to get online. If we had a stop for more than 10 minutes I'd go into the depot – none of them very large – and ask for the password.

If the train pulled into a station to pick up passengers, refuel or re-water I made my way through the smokers to stretch my legs and catch some fresh air. But just as important I was trying to fetch a signal. I could see my chances were not good in a tiny station called Rivers, Manitoba that closed a few years ago. Now it operates as a flag station. But since we were stopping to let a freight train pass, I got off anyway to look for a signal, just a few bars, just in case.

It was when I walked around the shuttered concrete and brick building stretching my legs that I saw two other people from the train.

"Hey, I like that smell," I said, picking up the telltale fragrance of marijuana, trying to be friendly.

"Wanna hit?" asked a tall bearded man.

"Sure."

"All right, mama," he said. "You go, girl."

Maybe it's the population difference between Canada and the United States – 37 million versus 325 million – but during the trip I couldn't help but notice how many fewer small towns – and exceptional depots – we passed through compared to the States. Some were strange. I had looked forward to Sioux Lookout, Ontario, based on nothing but the sound of the town. But all I saw was a small building shared by a modest depot, an osteopath and an optometrist. I had high hopes for Saskatoon. I liked the name. Again, a one-story bland building. There was nothing special in Edmonton, either.

One night – day three – I even held off eating on the train, thinking the 60-minute stop in Winnipeg would present a viable restaurant. The architecture proved interesting but not the timing. According to the schedule we were supposed to pull in around 7 at night, but freight trains – again – threw us off. I did get off the train, even if it was 1 a.m.; I'm glad I did. Another gorgeous

Beaux-Arts design with an enormous rotunda, finished in 1911. But I was too late – or too early – to see the Winnipeg museum. Another time.

The lakes and forests of Ontario, while beautiful and spacious, seemed to go on forever, much like Canada. Back to my book, Anne Enright's *The Gathering*, where her character Veronica ponders, "There were long stretches where I don't know what I'm doing or what I have done."

That sentence stopped me. I pushed the pause button. The sentiment seemed mighty appropriate for my affinity toward trains and for my life. It was nice to see it in writing.

CHAPTER SIXTEEN
TRAIN MEDITATION

BAKER WENT HOME three weeks ago, pulling that pink owl-themed suitcase behind her, safe and sound, no harm done. Baker is five. And now I'm leaving town. By myself. I'm sitting in the train station in Savannah with a small crowd waiting for the southbound Silver Star. The train is late. I'm going to St. Petersburg, Florida. I want to check out the Salvador Dali Museum. I've lived in Savannah for over 25 years and I've never been there. It's time.

For one week in July, Baker, Cara's five-year-old granddaughter (and mine by proxy), stayed at our house so she could go to summer day camp. The camp is an easy 15-minute drive from our house. Her parents live 30 minutes from town, so letting her sleep at our house for the week just seemed easier. It made sense. She sleeps over a lot. She has her own toothbrush, her own toothpaste, her own soap and shampoo, an extra jacket, socks, a special drinking glass, a box of crayons, an easel, a rainbow pillow and a bed, the chaise longue in our bedroom. She knows the house, and us, well. Her mom has prepped her well. Her dad, too.

For me the Dali museum is a good excuse to get away. What better way to go than by train? I could have driven. That's what I used to do when I needed a change. St. Pete is not that far from Savannah. But driving isn't as much fun as it once was. Too many cars on the road. Too many big cars you can't see over or around. I probably could have found someone to go with me but sometimes it's empowering to go off by yourself.

Also, it's not as much fun staying in motels as it used to be, especially by myself. The rooms smell of disinfectant. The nonsmoking rooms are suspicious. The pillows are either too flat or too thick. The bedspreads are slippery. The heating and air conditioning system is harsh; that's good when people are partying or zooming up on motorcycles and you need the white noise, but bad when the system wakes you up in the middle of the night as it kicks on.

But this time I was looking forward to being alone, even if it meant staying in a motel.

Now I'm outside on the platform. The train is close. A group of twenty-somethings just skipped by me, all happy with their young selves. They look alike. Same length hairdo. Same pants. Same purses. I wonder where they're going. The platform isn't that narrow but one of them could have looked my way or at least acknowledged me while passing by. Is that old-fashioned to think that way? What's so hard about a hello?

They make me cross.

The bigger issue is this: They don't see me. They don't see older people. We're invisible to them. Older people, in their eyes, don't exist. Is it the red splotches on my arms? Is that what does it? At first, I thought the spots came from getting poked by some branches while working in the garden. Now I hear they're the result of taking Tylenol or one of those other pain-killing drugs that might thin your blood in the process. But we love those drugs. They reduce the pain, they help us sleep. Wearing long sleeves to garden might be the answer.

My mind drifts back to Baker.

For a minute, I forget she left us and I wonder where she is. Oh, yeah, she went home. Our responsibilities are over. I panic when I don't see her. I think I hear her saying, "I'm hungry," or, "There's a stone in my shoe," or "The strap on my sandal is messed up." I remember I was supposed to get her a Band-Aid. It slipped my mind.

"Guess what?" Baker says when she walks in the house, pulling behind her the rolling suitcase we bought her last Christmas. "I'll be with you guys five days!" Then she holds up five fingers. "Guys" is such a Midwestern word. In the South, it's "y'all." Her parents must say "guys." I never noticed.

This was the plan: We would take her to camp in the morning, pick her up in the afternoon, bathe her, feed her, launder the special camp T-shirt she would need, unravel and dry the swimsuit, and then do it all again the next day. I have never had children, never especially wanted them. I like children. I play with children. I enjoy children. But I've never birthed or raised them. I like to say, "I don't know nothin' 'bout birthin' no babies."

Does it really matter if she brushes her teeth with "grownup" toothpaste?

Eight-hour segments, that's all I can claim by myself. But mostly three or four hours at a time. Then she and her little brother Benny are gone. Then my shoulders drop a few inches and I do what I want. Eat ice cream out of the carton. Ride my bike. Walk outside barefoot. Read without interruption. Go to bed without a light on.

Every morning before camp it was the same last-minute drill. Where's her lunch bucket? Did someone remember to make her lunch? What did we do with her water bottle? She needs her water bottle. Did we pack sunscreen? Does she need to go potty, one more time? Did we include her swimsuit? Is it the right swimsuit? Is this the day she's supposed to wear certain colors?

Hurry up! We're supposed to be there in fifteen minutes. The drawbridge could be up. Maybe there's an accident. Maybe there's a bunch of traffic. We have to allow for traffic.

But here's the deal: The worry, it seems, falls to me. No one else appears concerned. If I were in charge I would have all these things covered.

How do parents do this day in, day out?

In the afternoon after we picked her up from camp, she and I would go on one of our nature walks. I was determined to keep her away from the screen, any screen. She's OK with that as long as you divert her attention. The last time we were alone she wanted to watch a movie. I told her I didn't know which control to use. She told me to look it up, "Google it." She wanted to play a game on my phone. I had to say I didn't know how to do that, either.

"Well, then let's play Barbie," she said.

I wasn't really sure how to do that, but we got on the floor and I faked it.

Before we got to the park, she wanted to run on the sidewalk. Why wouldn't she? She's five; she hasn't been ambulatory that long, let alone able to run, to gallop, to skip, to dart this way and that. She has a great running style, knees, ankles, feet, all tip-top. I want to say, "Don't run. You'll trip. Pay attention. You'll fall on your head and crack open your lip."

I refrain.

Then she says she wants to take her scooter to the park. I feel myself getting a little impatient, but I say OK. We go back and get the scooter. I start to say, "Be careful of the cracks in the sidewalk. It's not very smooth. Look where you're going or you'll fall."

I hold back.

We went to the park because the days are long and she wanted some more play time. She always likes to go to the park. She hurried up the metal steps to the top of the slide. I get nervous and want to say, "Not so high. Be careful. You might fall through the steps. It could happen, you know."

I bite my tongue.

When another little girl came up and they started running around, racing, round and round, I start to say, "Don't overdo it. You'll get overheated." What exactly does "overheated" mean? My mother always said that to me. Now I am thinking it. We are well within the middle of the grassy part of the park, nowhere near the street, but I'm remembering Barry Bernstein from my youth: Barry, who ran into the street, got run over and was left with one limp arm. I think, "Stay away from the street. Watch out for cars."

I stuff it.

The worries don't end. Back home I'm vexed with other things. I want her to drink water to stay hydrated – "one more glass" – to eat some fruit. "How 'bout a banana?" I look at the clock and want her to get to bed on time, to get a good night's sleep.

That's not all. When we drop her off in the morning and I watch her walk into the camp, I worry about her camp counselor. Will she like Baker? Will the teacher understand her words, her humor, her specialness? Will she think it was funny that Baker misspelled "fish" making it "phish," the band her mother loved?

I worry about the other kids. Will they bully her, poke her in the eye with a pencil, punch her in the nose, stick out a foot to make her trip, fail to cover their mouths when they cough and pass along their nasty germs? Will they make fun of her because she does have a kind of endearing lisp she'll probably outgrow? And sometimes she still sucks her thumb.

It was exhausting. When the week ended I stood in front of our house and watched her drive off with her mom. That's when I thought: I can relax. But I couldn't. We went to the beach on Tybee Island that night. As I walked into the ocean I thought of Baker. Where is she? Is she safe?

How do parents do this?

Days later, I continue to think she's still with us. I look around to make sure there are no tempting electrical sockets she'll stick her finger into, no sharp objects around. Where are the knives? Put away the knives.

At first when she left, I felt free. What's that Tom Petty song about feeling free, free falling?

I'm liberated, I'm off duty, but then I missed her. How do parents adapt, adjust, think about anything else when they have kids? What do they do with that worry when they see their children get into a car with someone else? My mind doesn't stop there. How does a parent survive the death of a child? I was 16 when my cousin Pat, who was my age, died in a car accident. She was driving a convertible and a scarf flew into her face, covering her eyes. I listened on the upstairs phone when my Aunt Trudy called my mom, who had picked up the receiver on the downstairs phone. I heard my aunt say, "Pat is gone."

That's all my mother needed to hear. She knew what those three words meant. I thought it meant Pat had run away.

"I'll be right over," my mom said. Whole relationships, whole lives, a family, changed forever in that instant. I watched it happen.

Not too far into the train trip to Florida, I go to the snack bar. I don't feel like having dinner. Maybe I'll have one of those little bottles of Scotch and a couple packages of smoked almonds. I'm standing next to someone who looks old, really old. His hair is thin, his fingers gnarled, his stomach ample, his face mottled. His eyes look tired. He's wearing orange sneakers.

While we chit-chat, I figure out he's younger than I am. He starts telling me how he got on the wrong train in Savannah and I think, "How did you do that? There are so few trains." But I keep it to myself. I remember the time I missed a train. I didn't make a big deal about it. I too have trouble with numbers, schedules, connections, rules. Tell me to cut ten onions, I'm happy. Let me mince a dozen cloves of garlic, julienne a sack of peppers, dice up some celery, I'm good. Let me be a prep cook for the rest of my life.

"It's so hard," he said, although by this time I had lost the thread of the conversation. What is hard (except for everything)?

That made me think of Baker again.

"Beebe," she says. (That's what she calls me.) "Can you help me with this button? It's so hard."

"Can you help me get my scooter up the front steps? It's so hard."

That phrase resonates. "It's so hard."

I live with a planner, a "social chairman." That helps my life, makes it not so hard.

"How about dinner next Thursday?" someone will ask. "Or a movie?"

"Talk to the social chairman," I answer.

Then I hear a voice, someone in real time.

"How many grandchildren do you have?"

Oh, that's right. I'm in conversation with someone.

It's a fair question. It's not the first time I've been asked this. Before I met Cara almost 20 years ago and before her daughter and son-in-law had two children, I'd have to answer, "None." No grands. No children. A dog. Two chickens. Worms in my vermicomposting bin.

I felt guilty saying, "None." Is this bad?

A few months ago, I deposited some rent checks in a neighborhood bank I frequent. I was feeling chatty that day. "From here I'm going to go to the country and weed for my son-in-law," I told the teller. "He's a farmer, an organic farmer."

"Oh," she said, surprised. "I didn't know you had any children."

I didn't tell her he was married to my girlfriend's daughter. I let her think I had a child. I was posing, pretending to be like your average 70-year-old. Every time I see her after that I've wanted to correct that impression. I don't.

This is where your mind goes when you're on a train, when you have no weeds to pull, bills to pay, dishes to wash, clothes to hang, 5-year-olds to take on nature walks, when you're passing tractor supply companies, muffler and transmission outfits, pawn shops, water towers, cell towers, boarded-up banks, day care centers. Trains are anchored to the land, just like grandchildren. I am somewhere in between.

I AM MUCH OBLIGED TO THE FOLLOWING FOR
ALL THEIR HELP:

CARMELA ALIFFI, AMY PAIGE CONDON, EUGENE DOWNS,
LUCILLA GARRETT, TOM GREENSFELDER, DANIEL SNYDER,
VIRGINIA CENTER FOR THE CREATIVE ARTS, THE HARD-
WORKING FOLKS AT AMTRAK (ESPECIALLY DELORIS), AND
ALL THE TRAVELERS ALONG THE WAY.